Disclaimer

The information included in this bo[...] [...] helpful information on the subjects discussed. This book is not meant to be used to diagnose or treat any medical condition. For diagnosis or treatment of any medical problem, consult your own doctor. The author and publisher are not responsible for any specific health or allergy needs that may require medical supervision and are not liable for any damages or negative consequences from any application, action, treatment or preparation, to anyone reading or following the information in this book. Links may change and any references included are provided for informational purposes only.

Bitcoin

Starter's Complete Guide to Easily Buy, Invest and Trade with Bitcoin

By Susan Hollister
Copyright © 2019

Table of Contents

CHAPTER 5: ALL YOU NEED TO KNOW ABOUT WALLETS 65

Introduction

Congratulations, you have made a great decision in purchasing this easy-to-follow guide on how to buy, trade and invest with Bitcoin! You will also absolutely love all the incredible possibilities that Bitcoin offers. I've included everything you need to know to become comfortable with Bitcoin and to start using it like a pro.

To make the most of this new digital revolution, now bursting onto the world of commerce and finance, it is vital that you understand all things Bitcoin. This book will introduce you to the basics – and the many intricacies – of Bitcoin. I'll explain its background, describe the benefits you can expect to derive from it and reveal details that demonstrate how storing and investing works in the realm of Bitcoin.

How This Book Is Organized

You will find that this book explains everything in great detail in an easy to understand and fun way. The concept of cryptocurrencies is so new that it will take some explaining. It's also an incredibly complex topic, so we'll start out with a general overview that spans the first four chapters. This section will help you become familiar with the overall structure involving bitcoin, the blockchain, wallets and much more. These specific items will then be addressed in greater detail beginning in Chapter 5.

I'll also talk about business applications for Bitcoin, with due attention paid to international legal and tax implications. From there, the discussion will range from answers to skeptics to ways Bitcoin is being used today and what many anticipate is on the horizon. Of course, the issue of how to increase your wealth via Bitcoin will be woven throughout.

Bitcoin, The Game-Changer

We have all heard of cryptocurrency. In general terms, cryptocurrency refers to a digital form of currency that is encrypted online.

In 2009, the first cryptocurrency hit the headlines: Bitcoin. Bitcoin is a form of decentralized virtual currency. The "virtual" part means it's not attached to anything physical but exists solely as a mode of exchange agreed upon by the participants in its use.

By "decentralized," I mean that no single entity controls its existence. With all the hard currency we pass around daily, a sole authority oversees its production, control, distribution and value.   Cryptocurrencies, however, are different. They spread out the functions of controlling, accounting and currency production across multiple digital "nodes," so that no one entity has power over its value. Instead, the entire network supports this functionality. These new forms of currency have effectively removed the need for a single intermediary to be involved in their oversight. They also offer plenty of additional benefits that extend far beyond mere efficiency and ease of use.

With the disadvantages of individually-managed currencies becoming increasingly apparent, cryptocurrencies appear more attractive every day. This fresh concept of virtual currency is now in the process of taking the world by storm! Today it possesses the power to change both trading and commerce.

Can you see now why it's so vital to get a handle on the most powerful form of cryptocurrency on the market? Do you sense the urgency? Most of us are way behind the curve and have a lot of catching up to do. So let's dig in.

Chapter 1: All About Bitcoin

The aim of this chapter is to learn about Bitcoin, understand how it can benefit you and discover ways to keep yourself safe while amassing your own personal stash!

Obviously, you will be aware that Bitcoin is a new form of money known as a digital currency. But do you really know how it works? Let's start at the beginning, with the three major aspects of Bitcoin:

1. The origin of Bitcoin,
2. Bitcoin technology and how it works and
3. How you can apply bitcoin as currency.

By the time you finish this chapter, you will understand Bitcoin well enough to envision the ways Bitcoin can be of use to you.

Bitcoin's Origins

Bitcoin was the brainchild of Satoshi Nakamoto. Instead of designing an entirely new way to make payments and wipe out the way things can be paid for online, Satoshi looked for ways to handle existing problems within the current payment systems.

During the 2008 financial crisis, many individuals worldwide were affected by its impact on the economy. Today many people still suffer the ripple effects of that crisis on the value of their fiat currency. By the way, "fiat" refers to the government-approved official form of currency for a nation.

While the global financial system was on the verge of collapse, many central banks chose to attempt to ease the crisis by printing more money, a practice known as quantitative easing.

Quantitative Easing

As the central banks pumped money into the market to create liquidity, they also greatly reduced interest rates, intending to prevent a situation similar to the Great Depression of the 1930s. Their actions generated huge fluctuations in the country's currency values. It set off a flurry of currency wars, where nations raced to devalue their money and so make their economies stronger and more competitive than other countries.

The international response tends to be the same whenever this happens. Governments bail out their banks by printing additional money, ultimately devaluing the existing supply.

By helping the banks stay afloat, they bailed out some of the institutions whose reckless behavior had caused the crisis in the first place. The banks, who were apparently acting independently of their governments, guided many countries into unknown waters, without apparent concern that they were devaluing the nation's currency in the process.

The other choice was to let the country's economy collapse, putting it in the same situation as Iceland. When Iceland was unable to pay its debts, it experienced enormous economic instability.

A Third Option

Bitcoin offers a fresh way to think about money. It is easy to appreciate why some people are looking for creative new ways to establish a more stable economy. Because Bitcoin is transparent and decentralized, it offers an attractive alternative.

Welcome to the creation of Bitcoin, a financial organization with no connection to the few elite global decision makers. Satoshi Nakamoto decided the time was right for a different type of monetary system, a system that was different from anything currently in existence.

We don't know if Bitcoin was initially intended as a replacement for the current financial systems. However, we do know that many financial institutions are currently researching Bitcoin's technology with an eye to potentially adopting something similar for their own use. Of course, they are free to do this. The basis for Bitcoin technology, the blockchain code, has been open sourced from the beginning. Anyone can make improvements, even building whole new platforms based upon this code.

This innovation is about far more than using digital currency to pay for goods. Along with Bitcoin, the world-shaping development of blockchain technology has yet to be fully tapped.

There are many arguments about the flaws in the mainstream financial sector and any alternative is always to be welcomed. Whether Bitcoin will emerge as the alternative of choice is yet to be seen, but as the very first cryptocurrency to come out, it has great brand awareness around the world, which is a huge advantage.

Be sure to keep in mind that decentralization plays a significant role in Bitcoin. Bitcoin relies on no one: no bank, no government and no middleman. It was formed as a true peer-to-peer network in which each user doubles as part owner.

If there were no individual users, there would be no Bitcoin. The more people who embrace Bitcoin technology, the better it will work. Bitcoin depends on an ever-increasing community of people who are actively using the currency. Whether they use bitcoin to pay for goods or services, or they offer their products or services in exchange for bitcoin, active use is critical.

Digital currencies are a free market; therefore, anyone has the capability of setting up their own business anywhere across the globe and accepting bitcoin as legal tender. Processing a transaction takes a matter of minutes. Existing companies can add bitcoin as an additional method of payment, allowing them to grow swiftly from a local business to a national firm and then to expand rapidly across the worldwide market.

What's So Cool About Bitcoin?

It's almost an understatement to say the technology that powers Bitcoin is phenomenal. Bitcoin's blockchain technology is a completely new way of processing information. It is also a powerful and vital tool within the financial sector. This is not surprising, as most of Bitcoin's focus revolves around currency.

The technology behind Bitcoin provides users with options like never before. A massive amount of potential remains hidden and the best minds in the world are working to discover exactly what it will mean to see the Bitcoin technology integrated into daily life.

There is no question that the technology behind Bitcoin is seriously underestimated; however, it does have a slightly checkered past. Many platforms have been built with the sole aim of making it easier for people to use bitcoin. Unfortunately, this has not always ended well, especially in the realm of security. This type of technology involves extensive learning to understand it clearly.

The truth remains that Bitcoin is still maturing. It's young and experiencing growing pains, but we've only scratched the surface of its marvelous potential. The raw capacity behind this technology has caught the attention of a multitude of interested parties, with the forerunners coming from the financial sector.

There is much curiosity regarding the open ledger aspect of Bitcoin. Open ledger means the whole network can be viewed anytime by any individual from any location in the world. Anyone can watch transactions as they take place. While this idea may appear frightening, there are massive benefits to using a ledger that allows us to trace multiple events. None of the implementations need to be financial in nature, but a multitude of items in the financial sector are worth exploring.

There is still a lot to be investigated before you settle upon Bitcoin as a definitive method of sending and receiving payments. The decision to accept bitcoin payments on your virtual store will take only a few moments, but there are multiple implications when it comes to brick and mortar stores. You'll find many processors will happily assist you in exchanging between bitcoin and your local currency. The main advantages are that the processing takes a lot less time and it costs a lot less than working with credit cards or PayPal!

Bitcoin's Value

Whenever people talk about Bitcoin, the first thing they bring up is the price. Currently, the rate hovers around $6000 per bitcoin. Until 2011, bitcoin had very little value and when it began to increase in price, it was a slow process. In 2013, the bitcoin value peaked at just above $1,100;

however, many believe this was because of manipulation of the biggest Bitcoin exchange at the time.

The bitcoin rate is determined by its usage and by the concept of supply and demand. Although the bitcoin supply has been limited to 21 million, experts predict this will run out by the year 2040. Nobody knows why Bitcoin has been capped at 21 million, although some believe it is related the mathematical equations involved in generating bitcoin.

We have yet to see how the bitcoin value will behave when it is more commonly used. Even though Bitcoin has been well publicized, it is still a relatively unknown quantity. We expect it to emerge from obscurity, however, as the product matures.

Worldwide financial experts view Bitcoin as a pure form of digital currency. As we get our heads around this new technology, who can say whether this term is correct? We can conclude that Bitcoin is a valid way for people to pay for purchases and this makes the digital aspect increasingly appealing. There is yet more to explore and learn, about the potential uses of Bitcoin technology.

Bitcoin gives everyone - anywhere they are in the world - the opportunity to accept a common digital currency as a form of payment. Bitcoin remains the same everywhere, so it can be converted to any form of local currency upon request. There is no transaction fee and payments are received the very next day.

Mobile payments are increasing at a rapid rate. This adds another reason for choosing Bitcoin. It is an excellent source for mobile payments, giving businesses the ability to expand beyond national borders, at a minimal cost. Bitcoin is also an excellent investment tool if you're looking to trade in digital currency. More about this later.

Customers Drive Acceptance

Bitcoin needs to be used a lot more frequently for it to be recognized as a bona fide form of currency. Many sellers have yet to embrace Bitcoin and few buyers even know about it. As a result, it often falls on the shoulders of the Bitcoin user, to convince the other party of its merits.

The advantages for sellers are apparent: Bitcoin allows them to save on fees and other costs associated with payments. But this is only of value if customers use bitcoin to make payments. It really is up to the customers to make Bitcoin their preferred method of payment.

To make Bitcoin more convenient for buyers, a seller can offer the more familiar plastic in the form of pre-paid bitcoin cards or debit bitcoin cards. Both cards can have bitcoin deposited onto them. They can also be linked to a Bitcoin wallet, allowing the consumer to buy and sell bitcoin wherever they are accepted. Merchants pay the usual fees and receive payment in their own local currency.

While Bitcoin is far from being classified as a popular mainstream method of payment, I feel that now is the right time for people to begin using it as their go-to form of payment, even if only for the security of leaving cash and bank cards at home. Because fraud remains a constant danger, the ability to make mobile phone payments using bitcoin is increasingly viewed as a more secure option.

Widespread acceptance of bitcoin is not going to happen overnight. Until it does, those who are already using Bitcoin will need to be patient. It's good enough, for now, to know that you are already ahead of the financial curve.

Bitcoin Boosts Business

All forward-thinking retailers should prepare to use Bitcoin payments for both brick and mortar and online stores. They don't need acquire any additional hardware in order to accept bitcoin payments. Digital sales can be transacted using the existing payment infrastructure. All you need is an Internet connection, something most retailers already have in place. I'll describe more details in later chapters.

There are many business advantages to bitcoin:
- Accepting Bitcoin payments will involve an almost nominal transaction fee, far less than the three to five percent fee per transaction that is commonly charged by credit card companies.

- Bitcoin payments can be cleared and in your account, ready to be spent, the very next day. You can choose your preferred form of currency and will only be charged a small fee for any conversion. Compared to other card transactions, where you are kept waiting for a week or more to receive your funds and you're charged a fee of 3%-5% for the privilege, you can see why Bitcoin is a winner on all fronts.
- Bitcoin never changes, regardless of where you go in the world.
- A bitcoin's value is calculated precisely, to the last decimal point. For example, if you trade in US dollars and you charge $11.99, Bitcoin makes it possible to charge 11.98765432. This might not seem significant today, but if the value of bitcoin were to skyrocket, the extra decimal places could make all the difference and set you up for accurate future pricing.
- By accepting bitcoin, you can grow your customer base globally and you won't need to constantly track the exchange rates on multiple currencies. Bitcoin remains stable throughout and will suffice as a standard international fair rate of exchange.
- Bitcoin-to-Bitcoin is the term used to indicate that Bitcoin will not lose its value while it is waiting to be converted.

Consumer Advantages

As a consumer, the benefits of Bitcoin are straightforward. The first benefit is that there is little need to carry cash around. Cash money has a habit of filling up your purse with notes and your pocket with change.

Because bitcoin are every bit as real as your bank card, you won't need to carry cash or a billfold full of plastic. The advantages are numerous:

- Never again will you need to rely on services provided by a government-backed financial institution. With Bitcoin, you can pay anyone, anywhere in the world.
- When you pay online using bitcoin, the transaction is processed immediately.
- Bitcoin is a borderless digital currency; it operates the same anywhere in the world.

Help For The Bankless

Bitcoin offers a genuine opportunity for the thousands of individuals who are currently unable to own a bank account. For example, there are several African countries where fewer than10% of the population has a bank account. Is this fair? I am beginning to view it as a human rights issue. In some areas of the world, even though citizens may have the legal right to own a bank account, some of the banks establish such strict regulations that the vast majority of people find a simple savings account beyond their reach.

Society is trending toward a cashless existence. More and more people now use debit or credit cards, as a form of payment, both on and offline. Making payments via mobile phone is another trend on the horizon. It may well usurp the place of plastic in a few years. Whether or not you realize it, your smartphone gives you the means to complete transactions using bitcoin; the technical basis has been available for years.

On the whole, people are just now beginning to grasp the full potential of blockchain technology. They have scarcely imagined how useful it will prove in the future. A blockchain can do almost everything, you just need to locate the correct pieces of information and link them together in the right way.

Using Bitcoin technology, you can:

- Transfer funds between individuals; it covers all aspects of a transaction.
- Send money in seconds, to any location in the world.
- Convert funds into any local currency.
- Live quite successfully without a bank account.

This last item makes Bitcoin extremely powerful in areas of the world where bank accounts are not easy to come by.

But What If?

What if you live in an area without reliable internet access? Even today, some services will let you send a text to any mobile phone in the world to complete digital transactions. Yet again, Bitcoin proves that it is an effective tool in both the underbanked and unbanked regions of the world.

Take a look at the Bitcoin network and you'll be impressed by its capabilities. Each transaction is recorded and visible at all times, giving the user total access to financial data worldwide. In addition, the blockchain lets a user track the origins of any payment and see its destination, even while the money is in transit. I would welcome this level of transparency in our current financial systems!

Is Bitcoin Anonymous?

Probably the most significant question that surrounds Bitcoin is whether it can indeed provide anonymity. The truth is: no, not entirely. However, some anonymity exists when using Bitcoin and digital currencies in general. It's up to you to decide if it's anonymous enough for you.

Using Bitcoin to move your funds around gives you complete anonymity. If you want, you can completely hide your identity by using a Bitcoin wallet address. Wallet addresses are constructed from a complicated set of numbers and letters, which ensures there is no way of knowing who or you are or where you are located. Therefore, Bitcoin offers a type of protection not found in most other forms of payment.

This is as anonymous as it gets. Because all Bitcoin wallet addresses are visible in a public ledger known as a blockchain. The blockchain tracks any outgoing and incoming transfers from any specific location at any time. In other words, if I sent you a single Bitcoin, anyone can observe the transaction taking place between Wallet A (mine) and Wallet B (yours). No one would know the identity of the persons attached to those wallets, but the transaction itself would be in full view.

The story changes slightly when Bitcoin exchanges are involved. The transfers that you make from your Bitcoin wallet to an exchange are visible, when they are made public. Anyone can view a transfer from your Bitcoin wallet to the address of the wallet being used for the transaction since these are listed publicly. However, when the time comes to sell your bitcoin, it becomes much harder to trace where the coins have gone.

Third-Party Anonymity

It is possible to remain anonymous with Bitcoin. Currently, this facility is not yet very user-friendly. Generally, if you are highly interested in anonymity, it suggests that you have something to hide. You could use online amenities such as a wallet to mix up your coins, taking them from a different address, without the possibility of the addresses being linked.

Since this technology is still in the emerging stages, there are risks. If you were to lose your coins, they would be gone forever. Yet, you don't need to start worrying about losing your coins with normal transactions. When we discuss how to manage your wallet, we'll address these concerns.

If you use an external service to anonymize your bitcoin, you basically return to the original problem. The whole idea behind Bitcoin, after all, is that there's no need to rely on any third party, be it a bank, middleman, or whomever. Trusting a third party takes the control out of your hands and essentially goes against the core value of Bitcoin.

How To Protect Your Privacy

It's up to you to protect your privacy, but if you get in the habit of following two basic practices you'll be pretty safe:
- For every transaction you make, create a new address.
- Avoid posting your wallet address anywhere.

How To Make A New Wallet

After you receive bitcoin from another user, you can assign the transaction a new wallet address, one that has no link to any addresses you own. This allows you to isolate transactions and take the first step to protect your privacy. How you choose to look after your funds, the type of Bitcoin client and operating system you are using could allow you to make change, using multiple addresses.

The easiest way to understand this is as follows: if you had 2 coins and spent half a coin, you would require 1.50 bitcoin in change. This money can then be sent to a new address. This address has no link to your original address or the new change address, even though all the steps can be traced by checking the blockchain.

Wallet Address Privacy

Another way you can protect your privacy is to ensure that you do not post your Bitcoin wallet address anywhere. Any time you announce this address on social media, you have voided your privacy. If your wallet address is uncovered and linked to you, you cannot restore your privacy, at least not with that wallet.

Fungibility

The term fungibility means that goods are interchangeable or can be substituted. This is perfect for Bitcoin.

Most governments in the world stick to their own system of currency in order to remain in control. Local currencies are issued by a central banking system and are centralized. If the country needs further funds, the bank turns on the printing press to engage in quantitative easing. This means the central bank can boost the liquidity of the economy whenever it sees fit.

Trusting Bitcoin

One of the most significant stumbling blocks of any new technology is the issue of trust. I remember when online purchasing first rolled out; it took a long time for some people to feel comfortable enough to risk using the new technology. Today, I seldom meet anyone who hesitates to pay by credit card online.

With regards to Bitcoin, trust needs to originate from both sides. Even though you can control your money all of the time, you also must have confidence that the rest of the network can be trusted. However, since the chances are slim that Bitcoin will disappear overnight, there's little need to trouble yourself with this issue. While nothing in life is certain, the Bitcoin network is so secure, thanks to multiple checks and balances and information duplicated throughout the nodes, that it is able to run without pause, continuously troubleshooting and fixing problems on the fly.

The concept behind Bitcoin is what people have the most difficulty trusting. Its decentralization can be compared to the way the Google search engine works. Millions of people use Google at the same time, but it never slows down. Google runs on so many separate servers that it's nearly impossible to bring down the entire system.

Decentralization brings another possible concern to the fore. Because the network is made up of many separate users and there is no one person or establishment overseeing it, we could easily imagine that Bitcoin will dissolve into chaos, taking your money with it.
This means you will not be reimbursed if anything goes wrong, there is no guarantee, once your bitcoin have either been spent or lost they cannot be recovered.

It's Like The Internet

How often have you heard the term, "if it ain't broke, don't fix it?" When the internet arrived in the early 90s people would never have believed it could become a household utility. It was useful only to geeks, but look at it now! Everyone is on the internet; it'd be hard to live without it.

In many respects, Bitcoin is similar to the internet; it's a technology that is new and possibly too advanced for its own good! Like the internet, Bitcoin is solving technical problems most of us haven't even imagined.

Just like the internet, it will take time, before Bitcoin becomes mainstream. Although many Bitcoin applications are in development, it will take time before they come into common use.

Still, many already trust Bitcoin's technology. The majority of the existing technology focuses on money, like the remittance market. Bitcoin technology means you can send funds to any region in the world with little or no expense. Establishments such as MoneyGram, Western Union and even banks will be faced with stiff competition from Bitcoin.

Bitcoin Transactions

No, bitcoin is not a traditional currency. It is an alternative digital form of payment. Yes, you are able to use it to buy and sell. However, particular criteria are missing for it to be labeled a "true currency." Nevertheless, many merchants trust bitcoin as a source of payment, accepting it side by side with traditional payment methods. Bitcoin is easily added as a payment option because its adoption involves no additional equipment and no added overhead.

Merchants can easily integrate bitcoin payments into their physical and online operations. Bitcoin transactions are easily and immediately transformed into your preferred currency and the money is deposited into your bank account on the following business day.

When it comes to the consumer, using bitcoin to pay for things means you do not have to carry any cash or use or bank cards. However, to obtain bitcoin, you will typically need to buy some. This obviously means you have to begin spending your own money, but later in this book, you will see there are ways to earn bitcoin that don't involve you investing money up front.

Chapter 2: Getting Your Hands On Bitcoin

Now it's time to uncover what you'll need in order to get started using virtual bitcoin. I'll explain how to secure your first bitcoin, how to store and spend it and various security steps you can take in order to keep it safe.

Before we begin, you'll want to set up one – if not both – of the following:

1. Download Bitcoin wallet software onto your computer. To download, visit https://Bitcoin.org/en/choose-your-wallet
2. Download similar software onto your mobile phone, using the same link. Coinbase is a popular app choice for mobile phone users.

Let's Begin!

The most obvious question is, "How can I get my hands on bitcoin?" While there are a wide variety of ways, the most obvious is to purchase them. But, where do you go to buy digital currency?

The short answer: to online platforms referred to as exchanges. These work in the same way an exchange office does, allowing you to use "real" money (in this case, dollars) to purchase bitcoin.

How To Register With An Exchange

A Bitcoin exchange is most likely a website. There are a few brick and mortar exchanges, but we'll discuss these later.

There is plenty of choice among the online exchange options. At this writing, more than 100 exchanges exist around the world; the exact number fluctuates, but it will give you an idea of what you'll be wading through to choose one for your first purchase.

You'll first want to look for exchanges that honor the form of currency that you use. If your country accepts multiple currencies, you'll probably want to eliminate the exchanges that don't honor these currencies. As things stand now, no single exchange can legally serve everyone worldwide. For a summary of exchanges that may help get you started, I suggest you check the list provided by Bitcoin.org.

The primary purpose of any Bitcoin exchange is to transfer your local currency to a digital form of exchange and vice versa. You can actually hold an account at a Bitcoin exchange without owning bitcoin.

The process for registering at a digital exchange is as follows:
1. Create a user account providing your basic information.
2. Activate your account using information in the email sent by that exchange.
3. Once your account becomes active, the registration process will start.

Although bitcoin is based on a transparent market created around the number of people wanting to buy and sell them, to complete bitcoin transactions, you'll need to be able to contact each other. To accomplish this, the majority of Bitcoin exchanges offer what's known as a *trade engine*. Trade engines match the orders from people wanting to sell with those who want to buy. Additional trading options exist, such as local peer-to-peer trades; we'll take a look at these later in the chapter.

When choosing an exchange, you'll want to remember that some of them are not set up to convert bitcoin into a currency other than your own. When you withdraw funds and deposit them into your bank, they will be converted to your own currency, even if the bank you use does not take foreign currency. You need to carry out your own research before you start making money transfers to ensure that you are happy with the risks involved.

Bitcoin are governed by laws and financial bodies that will require access to some of your information, including your:

- Name
- Address
- Phone number
- Country of residence

Most Bitcoin exchanges will also ask for your birth date as part of the verification and validation process. In order to use a Bitcoin exchange properly, you will be asked complete a "Know-Your-Customer" process, known as "KYC" in short. Although this may sound scary, it's no cause for concern. At the same time, you do need to submit some additional delicate information:

- Confirm your phone number – The first thing that a new user will need to do is verify their phone number. Most Bitcoin exchanges will send you a text that includes a unique code. You then need to enter the code in a specific area during the process of verification to prove you can legally access this mobile phone. This avenue will be used for emergencies or as part of the password recovery process.
- Personal Identification – This step is required to verify your identity. You will be asked to provide a copy of your personal identification. Depending on the exchange you are using, the required documents may include a simple copy or scan of a recent household bill in your name along with your driver's license or they may require you to submit an image of your passport or birth certificate.

  The extent of these requests depends upon how much you are expecting to trade through your Bitcoin exchange. More substantial amounts call for more stringent verification and will include more sensitive personal information.

This is just a sample of the items you'll be tasked with as a new user. When buying your first bitcoin, you'll be expected to prove your identity. After you hand over your various forms of identification, you will wait as long as it takes for Bitcoin to verify your documents. Most exchanges will need only a few hours to review your documentation, but some people have reported waiting for up to a week.

Exchange Rates

Bitcoin's rate of exchange can vary dramatically, especially when you are exchanging against your country's currency. Exchange rates depend partly on the time you process a trade.

There can be massive differences between exchange platforms. Each Bitcoin exchange will do things a little differently, but they all share one common trait: they are hungry to attract customers.

You'll find the business of Bitcoin exchanges incredibly competitive. In most cases, novice users are the largest untapped market, so don't be surprised at the attention you attract. At the same time, you'll want to look beyond the bells and whistles to ensure the exchange you decide to go with will give you the best conversion rates, the timeliest service and the best possible accessibility.

Use the following tips to secure the best exchange rates:

- When you are looking to transform your bitcoin into currency and vice versa, it is essential to check the current price of Bitcoin. Over the past few years, there has been a trend whereby exchanges are offering a fixed rate on the provision that the transaction completes at a specified time. If you fail to meet this criterion, you may discover your bitcoin exchanged for lower or higher than the quoted fixed price.
- Keep your eye on the exchange rate between Bitcoin and your local currency. You can sometimes make a profit by trading up; at least you can minimize your losses. You'll find online tools available to help you; each will provide charts very similar to those you will see in any typical currency exchange office.
- Keep in mind that a transaction fee will be assessed at some point during any exchange. Pay attention to when it's assessed and how much will be charged. The smaller exchanges tend to charge more to make up for their fewer transactions, while the larger exchanges can afford to lower their transaction charges. Some exchanges charge less when your trading volume is greater, since your transactions are helping their liquidity situation.

  Fees may also be applied when you withdraw your currency and place it in a bank account or when you use a credit card.

Exchange rates on Bitcoin exchanges are continually fluctuating, based on changes in supply and demand. Over the past few years, trading in

Bitcoin has rapidly increased with highest volume of trades taking place in China and America. Despite this, other local exchange rates around the world may increase when major Bitcoin markets are going down and vice versa.

Monitoring Exchange Rates

Depending on the platform you have chosen to use, there are several ways to see the current exchange rate for your bitcoin. If you are using a computer, you'll want to check the Bitcoin wisdom site. This is where you can find up-to-the-minute bitcoin exchange rates for most major currencies.

If you are a cell phone user, your mobile wallet app will most likely show the fiat currency rate next to the value of coins you are currently holding. This practice is brilliant, since it gives you an instant idea of what your coins are worth. Of course, you'll need an internet connection for the price to be current.

Peer-To-Peer Vs. Regular Exchanges

There are two Bitcoin exchanges currently in use; they are peer-to-peer exchanges and what I'll call "regular" exchanges.

The regular exchanges track transactions in an order book. In this book, they accumulate both buy and sell orders between individuals. The buyer and seller don't know who's on the other end of the transaction, letting all parties benefit from this consistent level of privacy and anonymity. Most people expect a high level of both security and privacy when they are exchanging between their own currency and bitcoin.

Originally Bitcoin was initiated so that regular people could make transactions. We refer to this as peer-to-peer transactions or, in the Bitcoin industry, "a one-to-one relationship." In this type of transaction, data that relates to whomever you are dealing with is always available, so you won't need to deal with several different parties during the course of the process. The information you receive can take many forms; you may even meet in person if you so choose.

Instead of using a form of ordering book to match buy and sell orders online, while also overseeing the funds in use on the platform, peer-to-peer exchange platforms connect the buyer with the seller, but they have no involvement in the transaction itself. This setup is best when you're dealing on a local level. There are several platforms where you can register an account and find other Bitcoin buyers/sellers within the area.

Understandably, some people will not be open to the idea of meeting in person. Some will insist on payment using more traditional methods. Depending on how you wish to trade, peer-to-peer may suit you better than a regular exchange.

Bitcoin Storage

When you use an exchange platform to store your bitcoin, you need to be aware that there are many security risks to take into consideration. By using an intermediary, you are going against the whole ethos and ideology of Bitcoin. While the regular exchanges trade in decentralized currency, the actual platforms function in the same way as banks. In this respect, they share the same central failure points that make them vulnerable and a potential target for attack. However, Bitcoin is constantly developing safer ways to protect your money.

Unfortunately, regular exchanges don't have a very reliable safety record worldwide, when it comes to storing digital currency. If you put your money in the bank, you have a certain level of guaranteed protection. However, with a Bitcoin exchange, there is no security; you will be basing your choices on raw trust.

By choosing to keep your bitcoin on an exchange platform, not only are you trusting that service to be available online 24/7; you also assume the service it provides will be reliable. In a nutshell, trust the exchange to provide an adequate level of protection. Don't be put off though as exchanges have upped their security and continue to do so, but you need to remember that nothing is one hundred percent secure.

Even with all the added security, you should not view the exchange as a wallet service. There are several ways you can store bitcoin that are more secure. Storing your Bitcoin in a regular exchange for a long time is not that secure, but if you are planning to transfer or spend them within a week, this is a reasonably safe way to keep them. Leaving Bitcoin for any longer and you will be putting yourself in a risky position. When you want to store your best coins, the best choice you can make is a wallet as you will have full control regardless of whether this is a cell phone or computer device.

Bitcoin was designed to give the user has full control over his or her money. With this in mind, no one should feel reliant on a third party to keep their bitcoin safe. Just remember to transfer your bitcoin from a regular exchange or wallet to your specified Bitcoin wallet software as soon as you can.

Two-Factor Authentication

Even if you have no intention of keeping your bitcoin on an exchange for long, there are ways to protect yourself further. Most non-Bitcoin online services require you to maintain a username and a password, hardly the best way to protect your private data.

It has become apparent that we need at least one additional layer of security on top of whatever is your current method of identification. Among the most popular ways to address this problem is with two-factor authentication, which requires further information to access your account. You can consider it a second

It is not that difficult for someone to uncover your username and password and this may not have anything to you no being careful enough. By enabling two-factor authentication, you are adding another security layer to protect yourself and your money.

You can use two-factor authentication in many ways, but not every platform will support them. The most common is Google Authentication, which you can install fairly easily on any mobile device. Once you have downloaded the application, you need to set up your new account.

The following steps need to be followed to set up your account:

1. Log on to the platform you wish to protect with two-factor authentication.
2. Use your mobile device's camera to scan in the QR code.
3. Use this code to link your authentication details to pair with the mobile device.

Whenever you access Google Authentication, the system sends an automatically generated two-factor authentication code to your cell phone. This code is only active for a short time but is provided to give you access to your account. When you input this unique key, the system will verify it before allowing you to log on.

While two-factor authentication sounds fine in theory, in practice you'll encounter some challenges. You'll want to discipline yourself to keep your mobile phone charged and on your person at all times. Otherwise, you won't be able to retrieve the necessary access code for your account.

At the same time, if your device is lost or stolen you will lose the authentication information. There are ways to transfer the authorization to another device. However, the process presents a considerable hassle. It's easier just to avoid losing your cell phone altogether.

You can also authenticate your account using other methods. You can download an authentication application from your device's app store. Unfortunately, all of these options will bar text messages, so you'll need to carry an extra device to verify who you are, making for another form of inconvenience.

Text message verification also has its downsides. If you're in an area where you can't receive a consistent signal, you won't be able to connect enough time to launch the two-factor authentication process. If you're in a foreign country, you may incur hefty international calling charges in the process of receiving your code.

No matter which way you go about it, I highly recommend you enable some form of two-factor authentication to protect your account. While you may view it as a big hassle, you might want to weigh it against the considerable hassle of *not* protecting yourself and your assets!

Liability

When it comes to risks and liability, the law is full of grey areas where Bitcoin exchanges are concerned. Consequently, much of the burden of responsibility rests on your shoulders. Bear in mind that Bitcoin is not regulated or governed in any way. Depending on you're location in the world, you also will be expected to honor the regulations of that region.

It's unclear who is liable if an exchange gets hacked or if it were to abruptly. The more respectable exchanges will provide you with financial protection up to a point. If your money disappears while being held by their platform, it will reimburse you, at least partially.

At the same time, keep in mind that an exchange is the weakest link in the Bitcoin environment; don't use it for long-term storage but only to hold bitcoin there for impending transactions. Ultimately, there is no guarantee that you will be able to retrieve your funds if there are problems, so use it with discretion

Any protection an exchange can offer may depend on where it is registered, based on the licensing requirements in the area. If an exchange ceases trading, the local laws will determine what options are available to you.

Generally, the more complex the licensing, the more protection it provides. No matter what, you'll want to verify the details of your chosen exchange and understand the extent of any protection they can offer you. Do what you can to minimize your chances of loss.

Unfortunately, your liability far outstrips the ability of the law to protect you. Cryptocurrencies are so new that legislators and regulators haven't begun to get a handle on them. There are, as yet, few legal precedents on which you can rely. While it may be theoretically possible to take legal action against an exchange, any lawsuit at this juncture will eat up huge chunks of your time, as well as your money.

Fortunately for us, most Bitcoin exchanges welcome third-party auditors; they are glad for anything that will authenticate their honesty. Auditors will verify the solvency of the exchange and can test the security measures that are in place.

However, this risk highlights the reason most people gravitate toward cryptocurrencies: they want to maintain control of their funds. Personal liability merely is one indication that you are taking into your own hands the responsibility for managing your own money.

Encrypt Your Coins

One of the significant aspects of the Bitcoin environment is security. After all, without adequate protection, your bitcoin could be stolen. The core developers of Bitcoin recognized this issue from the beginning and made it possible to encrypt your wallets through the use of a passphrase.

Your Passphrase

Once you enable a passphrase, you are putting a padlock on your coins. This form of security would protect your bitcoin, even if someone were to hack your account.

Your personal bitcoin information lives in your virtual wallet, in a digital file called wallet.dat. When you first establish a wallet, by default this file is not encrypted. I repeat: when you install the Bitcoin nothing is password protected. Anyone with access to your computer can spend your bitcoin. In keeping with the basic principles of Bitcoin, it's up to you to encrypt your wallet. I suggest that you get in the habit of setting up secure access as you add a new wallet.

Bitcoin Core Client's most recent version offers to add a passphrase to your wallet. External passphrase generating tools are available, most of which are free. When you use them, you'll log in using your passphrase whenever you wish to access your bitcoin or review your past transactions. By encrypting your wallet, you are effectively placing it into "spectator mode" where all you can see is your balance and any incoming transactions.

We advise anyone who uses Bitcoin to encrypt their Bitcoin client software by assigning a password. This password should be as difficult to guess as possible. You'll want to include both upper and lowercase letters, as well as symbols and numbers. However, make sure it's something you can remember since you'll need to use it each time you access your wallet.

The process for encrypting a mobile wallet is a little different. Most cell phone applications place the wallet software file protected with a PIN code onto your device. PIN codes are not as secure as encryption keys, but they still provide an adequate form of security. It is possible to encrypt mobile wallets too, should you wish.

Malware

Whether or not you choose to encrypt your wallet, you need to understand that you cannot guarantee total safety, regardless of how many protective methods you put in place. Most people using bitcoin will already have installed a form of antiviral software on their computer. However, as soon as you start saving financial information — including Bitcoin data — on your computer, it's time to add additional layers of security.

Computer users require constant protection from harmful software. It is not enough to merely rely on a single antivirus program, especially when you are using your computer to store your Bitcoin wallet. You will need anti-spyware and anti-malware as a matter of course. Many products labelled as antiviral contain additional features that will offer protection from many of the security threats you may come across on the internet.

Malware is a significant threat known to plague Bitcoin wallets. There are multiple forms of malware and you'll want to protect your bitcoin from all of them. Malware can spread across everything you do online. Your computer can become infected when you visit any site that contains adult content. Clicking the wrong links on the internet, opening attachments on suspicious emails, or downloading content that is deemed illegal can all pose a serious threat to both your computer and your wallet.

Please don't let this make you paranoid; not all emails include malicious content. However, if you don't know the sender, you'd be wise to delete the message without opening it. For sure don't open any attachment it contains.

Blatant grammatical errors in supposed business communications are often an indication of danger. Suspicious links on your social media pages hold potential risk as well; just use your common sense and think before you click.

Spyware is another threat to your bitcoin wallet's security. It doesn't necessarily harm your computer, but it performs a more insidious function. It logs all sorts of information, such as website login details (yes, passwords), the type of software on your computer, even tracking the emails you have sent and received. If you are using Bitcoin services, spyware has the capacity to access your id and password. So much for security!

The good news is that you can install some pretty powerful anti-spyware and anti-malware software for your protection. You won't get it for nothing, but most software companies will provide a free test period so you can enjoy immediate protection while you're deciding on the best way to defeat these threats over the long term.

If you are taking the time to control your finances using Bitcoin, security is the most important concept for you to take on board.

Storing Bitcoin

There is an additional bitcoin storage option in common use by digital currency owners. This may surprise you, but it is possible to purchase actual, physical bitcoin.

Just as common currency comes in a variety of denominations, so do physical bitcoin. Each denomination of bitcoin is produced using a specific metal alloy that determines its value. The most common of the physical bitcoin are made from silver. You will also find bronze and gold bitcoin, each with their own denomination designation. The physical coins require an upfront investment and can be considered a collector's item or referred to as a Bitcoin vault.

You can store most physical bitcoin in a wallet address with a private key that is hidden in the furthest end of the coin. By doing this you are funding the coin by submitting a Bitcoin amount to the chosen address. All coins are supplied complete with funding instructions. Should you need funding information, check the small print. To use them, you'll be required to generate the address and private key, so you'll want to be the only person with access to this information.

Once you have generated the address and related key you'll be sent – along with the coin – a piece of paper with the confirmation recorded on it. The coin has a hologram that fits over the back of the Bitcoin. As long as this seal remains intact, you can be sure that your wallet details have not been compromised.

Most people store some spare bitcoin in the form of physical coins, hoping that their value will increase. There is no way these coins can be spent unless the hologram is broken to retrieve the private key.

Buying Bitcoin

A good way to get started with digital currency is to buy bitcoin in person. If you buy in person you can become familiar with peer-to-peer transfers. It is also an excellent way to meet like-minded people. You'll want to be cautious though; this form of Bitcoin transactions can attract unwanted attention. Thieves are increasingly aware of Bitcoin trades taking place face to face; anyone walking around with a sizeable wad of cash is an ideal target, so be careful.

Your Wallet

Prior to completing peer-to-peer trades there are some things you need to prepare. The most critical aspect of Bitcoin trading is the creation of your wallet address; with no wallet you have no way to store your bitcoin. You'll learn more about wallets in Chapter 5, but this will serve as a general explanation.

Your wallet identifier is a random selection of uppercase and lowercase letters and numerals that are pretty hard to commit to memory; that's for additional security. If your Bitcoin address were common knowledge, anybody could tap into all the information about you and your real-time activities.

It is possible to create Bitcoin addresses in several ways, however if you are completing a peer-to-peer trade, a mobile solution is probably your best bet. When you install a cell phone wallet app the address is usually created for you. Before you can use your chosen app you'll need to register it. As soon as you've installed the Bitcoin software, the wallet address is generated.

After everything has been created there is just one more thing to do. When you process a peer-to-peer transaction you will need to provide your wallet address to the other party. Rather than providing a string of random letters and numbers you can simply provide your QR code. Chances are you have seen the strange looking squares with black and white marks on a package or product. These QR codes are used by the banking industry to approve payments in stores. It's also an excellent way to share Bitcoin payment information with other people.

When you have created a QR code it is easy to share your Bitcoin payment details with others. The other party can use a phone to scan this code into their Bitcoin wallet application. With this, all the details required to complete the transaction will be filled in automatically on their end. The use of QR codes is user-friendly, time-saving and it improves the whole experience. QR codes can also provide up-to-the-minute information that permits a seller to prove to the buyer that the sale has been completed; when they check, the money will have appeared. Each normal Bitcoin transaction must be confirmed by six separate networks before it can officially take place, so the QR code can shorten that process.

In ten minutes intervals, a new block is released into the Bitcoin network and a transaction is then confirmed. Each time a block appears on the network, a sale receives a single confirmation. There are cases where it can take up to sixty minutes for a Bitcoin transaction to receive enough confirmations to become spendable. Some forms of Bitcoin wallet software will ready transactions for acceptance more quickly than others, particularly on mobile devices.

Meet In Public

The best place to meet for a peer-to-peer Bitcoin trade is in public. This protects both parties. It is always easy to find a public spot that is suitable for everyone. When you pick a public space, you'll want to select a location where you feel safe. You'll also want choose a spot that is in no way linked directly to you.

While most Bitcoin traders are genuine, you can never be 100% sure. Trading bitcoin via peer-to-peer meeting will always carry a small amount of risk, but it's not too different from meeting a stranger to transact a sale on Craigslist. In other words, while you will want to be careful in your transactions, people do this successfully every day; you can as well.

Premium Rates

One major downside to buying bitcoin in person is that you may end up paying a premium for the privilege, as opposed to the actual exchange rate. You should always check the current value prior to agreeing to a peer-to-peer trade; many bitcoin traders will not be aware of the current bitcoin value. Checking the current rate of exchange will also help you become comfortable with the way the market works.

The exchange rate for bitcoin can also work to your advantage. Because Bitcoin provides a free market that is based solely upon supply and demand, there's nothing to keep you from charging whatever you choose. Although buyers will want to pay the cheapest price, they will often be willing to pay slightly more for the convenience of a live trade. As a rule of thumb, you should always be prepared to pay a little more than the current exchange rate to get bitcoin, but this is a small price to pay to avoid the long, complicated verification process.

Payment Method

Choosing to make a peer-to-peer Bitcoin purchase provides you with far more payment options. You will usually agree upon the method of payment when you plan the details of meeting up for the transaction. Most often, the payment method will be cash money. You may also find local sellers who accept bank transfers, but this method is rarely used today. For a peer-to-peer trade no one will even consider taking PayPal or payment using a credit card because both of these methods can be used to charge back funds.

Cold Storage, Hot Wallets

These two phrases refer to security measures put in place to prevent mishaps with users' funds. Cold storage refers to bitcoin that are stored offline. The simplest real-world example is a bank that moves its customers' money into a vault at the end of the day, instead of leaving it in the cashier's drawer. Cold storage involves additional security layers. You can create cold storage by keeping your bitcoin on a USB drive or in a hardware wallet. Cold storage wallets are completely out of circulation. This protects them completely from hackers and computer-based security breaches.

A hot wallet refers to the way an exchange maintains a certain amount of liquidity to cover a huge amount of withdrawals. Hot wallets differ from cold storage in that they are always connected to the internet.

Keeping User Funds Safe

The top priority for any Bitcoin exchange is to keep user funds safe. A single loss by only one user would irreparably damage the reputation of the exchange.

To ensure protection of the customers' bitcoin, platforms use additional forms of security apart from cold storage. The need for other ways of securing virtual currency led concerned parties to develop of the Bitcoin Exchange Security Standard. This standard was established to oversee and improve the security of exchanges while also requiring the providers of wallets to meet a minimum standard that every platform must follow. In the past, sadly, not all exchanges focused on security, leaving many user funds vulnerable to theft and fraud. This standard is an attempt to raise the quality of these independent exchanges.

As you can see, Bitcoin is far from a perfect solution. It is growing, evolving and improving, but as I've mentioned repeatedly, the system is hardly risk free. Still, cryptocurrency is an idea whose time has come. Before long, it will be commonplace around the world, so it makes sense to explore both its strengths and weakness and learn to avoid the latter as you navigate the landscape. This is what we'll explore in the next chapter.

Chapter 3: Strengths And Weaknesses

If you are considering Bitcoin and weighing its strengths and weaknesses, this chapter will help you decide whether its benefits really do outweigh its negatives.

Bitcoin's Positives

1. Bitcoin is decentralized – it operates on a peer-to-peer blockchain as opposed to a central authority, making it immune to manipulation. No entity or person, not even Bitcoin founder Satoshi Nakamoto can make a single policy or change any information or the source code that Bitcoin uses. This means that Bitcoin can only work within a supply-and-demand ethos. This is what makes it more practical than centralized currencies.
2. Bitcoin is a trustless system. Both ends of a transaction are protected by the verification process of the system. Both parties are trusting not each other but the safeguards of the system to ensure that transactions are processed correctly.
3. Because the information is made public to everyone on the blockchain (more about that later) and because it's also verified using a proof-of-work protocol, the network is failsafe without any involvement by a third party. Since the birth of Bitcoin in 2009, it has never required a third party to referee any kind of dispute. With Bitcoin, you may need to trust a third-party wallet, but the blockchain has consistently proved itself.
4. Because it is a trustless system, there are no middlemen or third parties to take their "cut" from any transaction. In conventional life, when you buy something with your credit card, you are trusting the credit card company to take internal measures to guarantee that you will not be charged for something twice and that the company is operating in an ethical manner. You are trusting that the right amount will be charged and that it will end up in the correct place. Of course, you are expected to pay them for this service. I won't deny that fees still appear in Bitcoin transactions, but they're much lower than the fees associated with other methods of payment. We'll talk more about this a little later.

5. The trustless nature of the blockchain is so powerful that Vitaly Buterin, a programmer who worked on developing the software, extended the idea to create the concept of smart contracts. Smart contracts are enforceable digital contracts held on a blockchain. For example, imagine you are paying a premium to an insurance company for a health insurance policy via a smart contract. If you had an accident and needed to spend a few days in hospital, instead of your insurance broker trying to negotiate the insurance company's payments, the smart contract has the ability to release a specified amount of money to cover your hospital stay. This means no angry telephone calls while you wait for the insurance company to pay what they owe. It's a win for the patient, the insurance company and the healthcare providers.

   Buterin was able to use smart contracts to develop a blockchain network that allowed developers to design their own apps. The full potential of these trustless smart contracts is almost endless, as is the inhibition for corruption by anyone involved.

6. Bitcoin can be set up easily – It can be exhausting to set up an account with a bank or to get a new credit card. You need to go to the website, wait in a long line of, fill out numerous forms and then hope that your account is approved. After you gave the institution all sorts of personal information, if the company's security system is compromised, you will experience the anxiety that comes from the potential invasion of your privacy.

   By contrast, it's incredibly easy to begin with Bitcoin. To buy bitcoin, you need to set up a wallet and connect with one of the Bitcoin exchanges. First, you'll choose the type of wallet you want. Go to the wallet's home page, download a wallet or order the hardware and create your account. As soon this is complete you are ready to use the wallet's exchange service in order to buy bitcoin.

7. Bitcoin is anonymous – Apart from being far easier to use than banks, Bitcoin is anonymous. You are not obliged to use your own name when setting up your Bitcoin account; as a matter of fact, many security experts will advise against it. There is no need to provide any personal information so there's no way your personal information can be compromised.

In addition to the anonymity provided by Bitcoin there are additional steps you can take to ensure that you remain anonymous. Avoid using thin wallets and always use a VPN when you are on the Bitcoin network. Employ as many addresses as possible and never link your bank account to your Bitcoin wallet.

8. Bitcoin transactions are transparent. No one expected Enron to fail but the lack of internal transparency allowed it to conceal problems for a long time.

   With Bitcoin, there is no worry because the whole network is transparent. Each and every transaction is visible to every part of the blockchain network. Anybody can login to see exactly what is happening at any moment. There is a 100% assurance that your money will be safe from unethical practices.

   Bitcoin's protocol requires at least 51% of the entire community to concur before any changes can be made. Even the core development team cannot make any changes without this consensus; that's how seriously Bitcoin takes the mandate for transparency.

9. Bitcoin fees are tiny – Many credit card companies charge the seller a transaction fee of $3.00 or more. While $3.00 may not seem much, if you visit six different shops, that would add up to a whopping $18.00 those shops pay in fees, not including the interest a credit company amasses in the process.

   The transaction fees guarantee that credit card companies make money. They are charged to the retailers and sometimes are factored into the retail price of goods.

   Compared to these charges, Bitcoin's fees are miniscule. Bitcoin fees are charged as a way of ensuring that data miners are rewarded fairly for the work they put in to ensure smooth processing of transactions. The average fee varies, but if you want your transaction to be processed in the next available block (approximately the next 10 minutes), you'll pay around $1.30. If you can wait for an additional 20 minutes the cost drops to something like $1.12. Because the purchaser pays the fees, not the seller, the cost of goods is not affected.

10. Bitcoin is (mostly) free from government regulation – There are very few laws that limit how Bitcoin can operate. Most Bitcoin investors view this as a solid advantage; the fewer fingers are in the pot, the more say the individual has in how his, or her, money is handled.

11. Better yet, very few governments have even started considering how to tax cryptocurrencies. The fact that Bitcoin is not regulated by any central government makes it more appealing to those who use it.

12. Bitcoin is fast – When you receive your bank statement have you ever found some recent purchases have not yet appeared? The delay in processing can make it a real challenge to keep a handle on your funds. However, transaction made using bitcoin are sometimes processed in as little as 10 minutes and they are reflected almost immediately.

13. Bitcoin cannot be retracted – Fraudsters make money by questioning goods and services they have received, contesting payments and getting money credited back to their account, money that is pulled out of yours. Fraud committed by people in this way is paid for by everyone else who holds accounts in the same bank. However, because of the way Bitcoin is set up, this form of fraud is prevented.

With bitcoin there is no actual way the money can be returned to the sender unless the transaction is returned by the recipient. Because bitcoin are unable to be retracted, it's pretty rare for fraud to occur.

The Negative Side Of Bitcoin

1. Bitcoin is obscure – Few people have heard about it and fewer understand what it is well enough to consider using it. How cryptocurrencies work is largely a mystery throughout the world. This includes the vast majority of businesses, many of which could actually benefit from its implementation as legal tender.

At the same time the concept of cryptocurrencies has attracted its share of detractors. A small cadre of reporters and economists are devoted to discrediting Bitcoin and pointing to negative events as hailing its demise.

This lack of understanding and awareness has had a dampening effect on the growth of Bitcoin.

2. Bitcoin is volatile and risky – All assets with a monetary value go through cycles of boom and bust. All investments fluctuate in value. Bitcoin has already seen its fair share of ups and downs in the market. Its fluctuations have been large in comparison to traditional currencies and investments, losing up to 85% of its value in a single day. It's this extreme volatility that has warned away many a potential investor.

The volatility experienced by Bitcoin was greatest during its early days when there were few users, so any type of event would quickly ripple across the entire system. For example, the value of Bitcoin plummeted steeply in 2012 after the American government shut down a Ponzi scheme known as Bitcoin Savings and Trust.

However, currently millions of people are actively participating in the Bitcoin network with trillions of dollars-worth of bitcoin in active circulation. While external events may still affect Bitcoin, they no longer shake the structure as strongly as earlier.

3. Bitcoin is still developing – Blockchain technology is still relatively new and the network is yet in the development phase. Programmers are continually adding to Bitcoin. There are undoubtedly unforeseen problems yet to emerge and be dealt with. The system may have emerged from its infancy, but it is now in toddlerhood, with all the upheaval and chaos that entails.

4. Bitcoin burns tons of energy. Number crunching has always been an energy hog and with Bitcoin the number crunching is on a scale never before seen. It is estimated that by 2020 Bitcoin will require as much energy as it would take to power the whole of Denmark. Bitcoin is increasingly challenged to find ways to reduce the energy used by the network without compromising security.

5. **Bitcoin is largely unregulated** – Yes, this is both a strength and a weakness. Because it is unregulated and its legal boundaries are as yet untested, some people shy away from these unknowns.

What if someone sued Bitcoin? Would the law look upon Bitcoin as a financial asset or merely an imaginary market? As of this moment, we actually do not know. What we do know is that, comparing all of 2017 to just the first three months of 2018, the number of American lawsuits involving cryptocurrencies tripled. Well, to be honest, there were only seven filed in 2017; and at least a third of the 2018 cases came from the Securities and Exchange Commission. At issue so far is not the Bitcoin network itself, but entities attached to the network, usually the exchanges.

Trends

When you think of the negatives, you might wonder if Bitcoin is worth your while. After all, there is a pretty steep learning curve in the offing. It might help to learn how well Bitcoin is faring overall.

Since its launch, Bitcoin has grown gradually but fairly steadily from about 300,000 people in 2009 to somewhere between three and five million users in America alone. Worldwide, about 20 million people access Bitcoin, scattered across about 40 countries.

The number of transactions processed daily has remained fairly stable over the past seven years or so. Since early 2017 however, the transaction count has been exploding. The people who own bitcoin are now using them to transact business and they're using them a lot!

Still, these transactions are a miniscule figure, compared to those processed by the credit card giants, even in comparison to PayPal. Around the world, less than five percent of the population owns any form of cryptocurrency.

Now you can see why I likened Bitcoin to a toddler. It has a lot of growing to do before it can take its place on the world's stage as a major player. Still, you can do a lot with Bitcoin even now. The next chapter will show you some ways you can actually make money using Bitcoin.

Chapter 4: What You Can Do With Bitcoin

There are four basic ways you can use bitcoin to make money: bitcoin mining, funding via bitcoin, earning bitcoin and trading it. While the most obvious method is to use it as an investment, there are many other ways to use it to increase your wealth. Surprisingly, some methods are not very costly. By the time we're finished here, you will know which money-making strategy is best for you.

Job Earnings

You can actually be employed on a job that will pay your salary in bitcoin. While this is only a consistent reality among employees of companies that are leading the development of cryptocurrencies, a Japanese internet company recently announced that it is giving employees the option to receive part or all of their salary in the form of bitcoin. So, it's beginning. Don't be surprised if you receive a similar offer somewhere down the line.

Where you are located will impact whether and how much of your Bitcoin job earnings are eligible for taxation. We'll discuss taxes and other legalities in greater detail in Chapter 10. For now, however, suffice it to say that the tax situation is different in each country, so you'll need to check with your local authorities to find what, if any, taxes apply to your bitcoin as well as your bitcoin transactions. In America, the tax authorities currently view bitcoin as property, not as equivalent to cash. This may complicate the process of providing payroll in bitcoin, but even this will probably be ironed out, eventually.

Bitcoin Trading

If you want to make money using digital currency the most straightforward way is by trading in bitcoin. Since the price of bitcoin is incredibly volatile, if you know what you're doing you can make a tidy profit by buying and selling bitcoin at the right time.

Over time, successful bitcoin trades can yield plenty of money, but things can also go terribly wrong; you can easily lose more than you gain. It is incredibly important to be fully aware of the risks involved in trading. Only invest money that you can afford to lose.

Day Trading Vs. Fiat Currency

Day trading is the term given to transactions bought and then sold in a single day. Fiat currency involves a national government's form of legal tender. There are several ways you can trade against fiat currency using bitcoin.

An obvious method is to exchange between bitcoin with the appropriate local currencies. Traders usually prefer the greatest currency markets, since they offer a better profit than smaller currencies. You should not be surprised to learn the principal trading market today is in China, where bitcoin can be traded against the Yuan.

Your ability to acquire Chinese Yuan for trading is determined by where you live. Contact a local bank to learn how you can get your hands on Chinese Yuan and to discover its current exchange rate.

It is easy to convert other currencies to or from bitcoin, because Bitcoin currency is now supported by many exchanges. If you already own your own bitcoin, you will not need any form of fiat currency to begin trading. Simply make a transfer using bitcoin into your preferred exchange and you will be ready to trade against any form of currency you wish. However, beware: because the bitcoin is highly volatile, there are both profits and losses to be made on a regular basis.

There are other options available that will allow you to trade on the Bitcoin and fiat currency market. Many platforms will display up-to-the minute information that will help you decide when to buy or sell against a specific market. Some of them will even accept payment in bitcoin. While some merchants will allow payment in bitcoin, most of them will have funds changed directly into the fiat currency. The reason is to protect the merchant against the volatility of bitcoin.

This is the primary reason many stores are joining the Bitcoin market. However, the exchange from bitcoin to the local currency can have the side-effect of creating major pressure to sell across major exchanges.

Bitcoin payment processors rush to liquidate payments as quickly as they can, so they can pay the seller the correct amount of money. This can result in many major bitcoin transactions occurring simultaneously. The result can appear in the form of optimal conditions for buying bitcoin at a lower rate than usual.

Bitcoin speculation is *not* something you should enter into lightly. The traditional influences on your fiat currency also impact the bitcoin price. You will also find, once you begin trading, that the bitcoin price can change for no apparent reason at all; both major upturns and significant losses can appear out of the blue, with no logical explanation.

Altcoins Vs. Day Trading

Now that you understand what constitutes day trading we will look into altcoins, a term for all the other cryptocurrencies that are not bitcoin. These are Bitcoin's rival siblings and, in some cases, Bitcoin clones. While we'll discuss altcoins in greater detail in Chapter 13, what follows will give you a general idea of how they can be used in trading.

Currently there are an excess of 1,600 different forms of altcoin in existence. If you have decided that trading on the bitcoin market against fiat currency is not for you, this is another alternative you have at your disposal. You can trade bitcoin against altcoins.

Altcoins are all trying to emerge as a better version of what Bitcoin stands for. Some altcoins offer greater anonymity than that offered by Bitcoin. Others are developed in order to probe the limits of the blockchain technology that underlies all cryptocurrencies. Instead of joining forces with existing Bitcoin developers, they create their own coins, using the original Bitcoin code, enhanced by their own alterations. These developers give the coin a new name and, presto, a new digital currency has hit the market.

At this writing, about fifteen altcoins have emerged as key frontrunners. These favored few are blessed by a community of loyal supporters. Their loyalty often lies with the unique features a particular altcoin possesses, usually features that aren't currently supported by Bitcoin.

If you choose to look into the world of altcoins, you'll quickly discover that their community is not as large nor as supportive as the Bitcoin community. However, this does not stop people from speculating in altcoins. They are often growing faster than Bitcoin, so it's easier to see greater profits with them. For this reason, day traders often prefer altcoin markets.

Altcoins tend to be created by developers who hype up their new coins with promises about unique and interesting features. When people first hear these statements there is a flurry of buying activity. Of course, this results in a steep increase in the price. There are plenty of altcoins for everyone and the majority never actually serve any kind of purpose. If you are lucky and buy some coins cheap before a price increase, you have a good chance of making a quick profit. Just don't hold on too long; the prices can plummet even faster!

Bitcoin And Crowdfunding

Crowdfunding operations allow you to decentralize your funding efforts by attracting your own investors and followers. You invite these participants to set in place the upfront money for you. By offering to receive contributions in bitcoin, you are further decentralizing your funds and can reach a far broader global audience than otherwise.

Thanks to Bitcoin, it is easier than ever before for businesses and individuals to raise funds. Bitcoin is untaxed in most countries, so many people view it as a way to enjoy tax-free investments. Yet, you will want to remember that when bitcoin is exchanged it may well be taxed at its destination.

If you choose to crowdfund, you'll want to be as transparent and honest as possible. Don't dare make any false claims or promises. While Bitcoin is an irreversible payment method, people *will* find you if you attempt to abscond with their money. Fortunately, the vast majority of crowdfunding so far has been trouble-free, with investors getting exactly what they were promised.

Most platforms do have security in place to prevent incorrect use. Regardless, there is always the possibility that a deal may not put forth exactly what it promised.If you choose to assist in a Bitcoin crowdfunding project, you should find out whether or not you can expect to receive a reward. Crowdfunding has nothing to do with buying shares or getting something at a knocked-down price. It simply means that you are happy to give someone else your money so that they can bring their dreams to fruition. When the dust settles, you may or may not receive something in return. Crowdfunding was never designed to reward the donor, so if you choose to participate it should be on the assumption that you will not see your funds again.

IPOs And ICOs

An initial coin offering (ICO) gives investors the opportunity to purchase some of the total altcoins prior to the start of the mining process. The majority of investors will take advantage of this opportunity in hope that the coin's value will increase.

Initial public offerings (IPOs) are used when a coin company wants to raise extra funds to assist with its operations. In this scenario, investors are given a share in the company and will earn interest that is returned via dividends.

Each of these terms carries a negative implication where Bitcoin crowdfunding is concerned. Unfortunately, many promises have been made and broken by bitcoin participants. In addition, numerous nefarious scams have been associated with IPOs and ICOs. The situation is not completely bleak, however. Both of these financial activities have been used for plenty of legitimate purposes as well, so please don't write them off entirely.

For example, if you plan to create a new usage for the technology behind the blockchain that will require its own coin (in this case we'll call it a token), you are setting up an ICO. Depending upon the amount invested, a user will receive a certain number of tokens to use on the platform, once it is up and running. This gives backers a form of reward, even if it's nothing physical. Any value their tokens gain is contingent upon the success of the venture.

It's not necessary to provide tokens to individuals who wish to invest in your project, although everyone likes to be rewarded for their contribution. The implementation of an ICO or an IPO can prove helpful for raising funds, especially when you have a clearly defined scope for your project.

Company Shares And Dividends

Instead of offering investors digital rewards, another strategy is to grant them shares in the project in exchange for their participation. The owner can set the value of the initial shares at anything they wish; just keep in mind that the shares *must* have some residual value. Company shares can be given value by offering quarterly, monthly, or weekly dividends to the investors. Investors like dividends and may well spread the word to their friends, leading to even more investors coming on board.

To improve upon the dividend idea, you could pay it out in bitcoin, or your form of token, although the amounts would be small in the beginning. Once the investors start reaping the rewards however, they'll be glad they took the plunge. When others see how well the company is doing and get a feel for the scope of its potential, you'll not only gain additional investors, you'll be building a positive reputation for yourself and your offerings.

Bitcoin For Your Future

Speculators worldwide are attracted by bitcoin for its short-term potential, but what about long-term investments? Will the cryptocurrency's wild price fluctuations turn to your advantage over the long haul?

On the one hand, you could make a tidy sum by buying at a low price and trusting in a future price hike. Since there will only ever be 21 million bitcoin in circulation it seems likely that the price will experience growth over time, but nothing is certain in this world.

It's highly unlikely that the bitcoin market will go belly-up in the near future. Yet, the currency is too new to provide any sort of long-term track record. We simply lack enough historical data to formulate any opinion regarding its future trajectory. While the future appears promising, I would be a fool to make any promises. I will offer you tools throughout this book that will help you in your decision-making process, but in the end, the decision is yours to make.

Forward Investing

Many consider Bitcoin an investment vehicle. At the birth of Bitcoin, people brought up cheap coins that were offered to boost its growth. By giving coins away, the price was bound to increase.

The value of Bitcoin has risen dramatically since its launch in 2009, when each bitcoin mined was worth next to nothing, quite literally. By the end of its first year, bitcoin's value was up to eight cents. It hovered around that spot for a long time, until the next year brought a fresh surge of interest in Bitcoin. As the concept of cryptocurrencies piqued the interest of increasing numbers of investors, the price began a slow and steady climb.

Suddenly, in 2017, the price of bitcoin skyrocketed. Bitcoin reached its all-time high to date on January 1, 2018, when the price per coin peaked at $15,127.51. However, this was an unsustainable level. Bitcoin plummeted for about nine months, eventually stabilizing near the $6,000 mark. Still, this is an astronomical improvement over its original value of $0.00008

Hodling

No, hodling is *not* a typo, although it began as one. The term describes a loyal bitcoin owner who is "Holding On for Dear Life" to his bitcoin, in spite of current downturns, in the nail-biting hope of its value rising across the long haul. This practice is not new; investors have always weighed holding versus selling when prices began to dip on long-term investments. What is unique to Bitcoin is the stubborn loyalty of some of its investors, who are determined to hang in there, no matter what.

Controversy is currently raging as to whether hodlers are helping or hindering the overall health of Bitcoin. Some investors believe that removing bitcoin from circulation in this way will actually boost the coins' value for everyone. A number of corporations are adopting this practice as a form of "insurance" against cyberattacks on the currency.

The opposition argues that the only way bitcoin will increase in value is by using it. In their minds, more individuals and businesses will commit to using bitcoin only as they see the coins increasingly in demand for everyday transactions. They view hodling as a destructive strategy that will bring bitcoin trading to a halt and reduce the value of the cryptocurrency to zero.

Hoarding Your Wealth

Many people have already made the decision to invest in Bitcoin. There is now an issue with investors who have purchased Bitcoin at a ridiculously low or extremely high price and are now sticking with their investment, hoping to either make their money back or see a profit. With so many bitcoin held onto for unknown periods of time, there are concerns about how bitcoin will fare in the future. With the price drifting horizontally instead of vertically, demand appears to have slowed down. However, the many people holding onto their coins could bring bitcoin, with one sale, back to pre-2018 prices, so the potential for growth remains.

With any type of investment there is risk; some people will grow impatient and liquidate their assets. Bitcoin is no different. It is a digital currency with a capped amount; a fixed number of coins is scheduled to enter circulation. That number is increasing gradually until the total of 21 million bitcoin have been released for use, sometime in the year 2140. Currently, about 70% of the circulating bitcoin are being actively traded. The remaining 30% are either lost (something like eight percent) or are being held by their owners and are neither sold nor used in transactions.

How To Earn Bitcoin

Trading and investing aren't the only ways to multiply your bitcoin. Instead of purchasing bitcoin from an exchange or trading them for a profit, you can earn them. Bitcoin can be earned in an abundance of different ways. Here we'll highlight a few.

Run A Signature Campaign

Discussions with regards to Bitcoin online usually take place on the Bitcoin Talk forum. This forum is an ideal place for new and established businesses to advertise their services. It is also an excellent way to boost your understanding of bitcoin

At the bottom of each contribution by forum participants is a signature. The forum allows likeminded people to talk about Bitcoin and earn a small fraction of a coin for each post they publish under their signature. The person who organizes the signature campaign tracks the number of posts each user publishes over an agreed amount of time and then pays the appropriate amount. While well-thought-out opinions or answers make up most of the posts, clearly stated questions can also count.

You are rewarded according the total number of posts you've published. It will take writing something like 125 blogposts in order to start seeing significant returns, but only slight risk is involved with this method of earning Bitcoin.

Visit A Faucet

Probably the simplest way to earn bitcoin is through visiting faucets. A faucet is a form of pay-to-click website (PTC) that allow users to earn a small amount of bitcoinage for clicking on ads found on their site. You won't get rich visiting faucets, but the work is simple and requires only the use of a personal computer with internet access.

Faucets will keep giving you small pieces of Bitcoin for responding to advertisements. Usually the people who operate the Bitcoin faucets will make payments until they have attracted enough visitors to the site and have sold some of the advertising space on their website. While this is a low-cost, low-risk way to spend your time, the yield is minimal; an entire day's work may earn you a dollar...if you're lucky. The real earnings come when you own a faucet.

Own Your Own Faucet

Running your own faucet could generate up to a thousand dollars a month. You'll put in plenty of work and some of your own money in the process of getting started. In addition, maintaining a successful faucet will take considerable time. However, the results can be significant.

Put On Your Writing Hat

If you're at all proficient with words and if you're interested at all in cryptocurrencies, you can make some decent money by writing blogs, articles and information pieces around the topic. The novelty of virtual currencies means that almost everyone is curious about them. There's a huge market right now for well-developed, factual articles and nuts-and-bolts how-to instructions for almost every aspect of Bitcoin and the myriad of related products and services that follow in its wake. It can be a challenge to keep on top of the constantly emerging new developments, but that's where the greatest need lies for competent writing, on the cutting edge.

The need is so great that you don't have to be a top-of-the-line blogger to get noticed. If you can explain something like data mining clearly enough that a 10-year-old can understand it, you'll find plenty of people who will want what you write. Hire a competent editor to clean up any technical issues and get to writing.

Build An Affiliate Link

Here is another low-risk method for earning your own bitcoin. It involves enrolling in affiliate programs for Bitcoin-related businesses. Each business assigns you an affiliate link, which you then use to send visitors to their site. When one of your visitors makes a purchase, you are paid a commission, in bitcoin.

Provide Supportive Services

Bitcoin and other cryptocurrencies have spawned a host of industries that support them. If you have site design, data manipulation, or number crunching skills, you will be in high demand. Thousands of people are out there, willing to pay you to work on their affiliate linking sites, design web pages, or program supportive software. For starters, you'll find a host of potential clients at the "Data Science & Analytics" category of Upwork.com, a major online hub where available jobs can find skilled workers.

How *Not* To Earn Bitcoin!

In your quest to multiply your Bitcoin holdings, you will come across all sorts of strategies that will each tout their offering as the "next sure thing." While some of them are legitimate, if they promise earnings that just appear too exciting to be true, they usually are. As with most online offers, it's all on you do your due diligence before committing your resources to any new strategy. Check scam listings, look for pending lawsuits and carefully search for truly independent reviews, before you commit to anything.

While some may seem obvious, here are a few ways to pursue more bitcoin that you should avoid.

Lending

Lending to individuals is always a risky venture; lending bitcoin is even more so. The chances you'll never see your money again are even greater than with regular currency, largely because of the anonymous nature of transactions.

Gambling

Yes, there are plenty of online bitcoin casinos. As with any form of gambling, the risks are so high that you should *never* commit any Bitcoin holdings that you *cannot* afford to live without.

At the same time, if you *must* gamble, you'll want to look for a bitcoin casino that is certified as "provably fair." This indicates that the site operates a truly random number generator and is not prone to favor any one client.

Mining

We'll discuss mining in greater detail in Chapter 8, but this will give you a general idea of its possibilities. In the beginning of Bitcoin, it was possible for an individual to harness their computer's central processing unit (CPU) and later its graphic processing unit (GPU), to perform the complex calculations necessary to create a bitcoin block. The difficulty has always been the huge amount of electricity it takes to churn out these calculations. Electricity generates heat, so cooling the unit also becomes an early challenge.

During Bitcoin's short history, the cost of the necessary hardware and the accompanying electricity and cooling demands have grown to the point that it is no longer feasible for an individual, sitting in their living room, to profitably run a mining operation. It's just too expensive.

Cloud Mining

In these systems you contribute money to pay the electricity charges and fund the necessary hardware for the cloud to do the mining for you. Because mining has become incredibly complicated, the chances of making a profit via cloud mining are now very slim.

Chapter 5: All You Need To Know About Wallets

When you purchase bitcoin through an exchange, you could technically leave all the information with the exchange, but that's not recommended because you don't have any control over the exchange. Instead, in order to remain in control of your bitcoin you'll want to transfer this digital information to a wallet. A bitcoin wallet is, as the name suggests, a safe place to stash the information relating to your bitcoin, while you're deciding where to spend it.

Your bitcoin wallet holds the private keys that identify you as the owner of your bitcoin. From your wallet, you can buy and spend bitcoin, just as you would move money to and from a physical wallet. Your bitcoin wallet is the vital holding place and the protector of your digital currency.

Using A Bitcoin Wallet

When you withdraw cash from an ATM, you usually put it straight into your purse or wallet. You'll want to do the same with your bitcoin. Bitcoin need to be stored somewhere that gives you access wherever and whenever you wish.

Your Bitcoin wallet is the same as a wallet that you keep in your pocket or your purse.
In a public ledger referred to as the blockchain the bitcoin are stored digitally. This is the software your bitcoin uses to communicate with the blockchain and allow you to see what you have at any given time. The blockchain is the nerve center for the Bitcoin platform.

Addresses

After you install your wallet, you can create as many Bitcoin addresses as you need. This is particularly useful since it gives you the opportunity to provide dedicated addresses to those who send bitcoin to you.

What's In A Wallet?

What we're really talking about is a software application. The app could reside on your computer, phone, tablet, or other digital device. It could also reside somewhere on the internet. It could live on a removable hard drive, or even a thumb drive, enabling it to be cold stored safely away from other digital sources.

With this software, you can create your own public wallet address or key. This is like a bank account number, your unique bitcoin identifier. You'll need it in order to receive, send and store your bitcoin. Your wallet also houses the private keys that are attached to your bitcoin. You need both in order to interact on the Bitcoin network.

The most common wallet types to date are:

- Paper wallets
- Hardware wallets
- Mobile wallets
- Web wallets

Paper Wallet

Paper wallets are, as their name implies, a way to store both your private and public Bitcoin keys on paper. You create paper wallets via a paper wallet generator. These programs actually generate keys on your own computer, so that none of your private information exists on the internet. They allow you to "play around" with the keys, moving your mouse around to add to the randomization of the keys.

The most common legitimate paper wallet generators as of this writing are:

- Walletgenerator.net
- Bitaddress.org

The keys are printed out and they are usually also provided in QR format, allowing you to scan them in order to perform transactions.

This method of cold storage is a bit controversial. Some people consider it obsolete, as in a couple years old. In their opinion, a paper wallet is about the most unsafe way you can "secure" your bitcoin because it involves printing out the information and storing it in paper form. Whenever you are using paper, it vastly increases the chances of someone else getting their grubby hands on your bitcoin. However, there are enough people who swear by paper wallets that it's worth considering. Paper wallets have the advantage of being impervious to hacking. The only way you can use the contents is to scan the QR code or manually enter the key into an online location. Paper wallets are quite popular, whether used temporarily or for the long term.

With paper wallets, their security rests squarely on your shoulders; your actions determine how "secure" are your bitcoin. And remember: if something happens to that piece of paper, say, it's damaged in a flood or your dog eats it –your private keys are lost forever; you're out of luck with no way chance of ever accessing them again. Without your keys you can't get at your bitcoin and it'll be unused forever, floating around the Bitcoin universe with no nope for reclamation.

You can minimize the risk of using paper wallets by adopting one or more of these practices:

- Ensure that you are offline when you generate your wallet. Some people go so far as to download the application from another computer onto a thumb drive, then install it on a computer that will never be connected to the internet and to generate keys that way. They also use a "dumb" printer, connected by cable to this computer, for printing.
- Print off three copies and store one in a safe deposit box, another in a home safe and the third with your attorney.
- Use printable plastic; it won't age or deteriorate like paper.
- Fold the paper in half so the private key is hidden.
- Affix a seal over the folded key; you can find seals that are "tamper evident" so nobody can open them and replace the seal without you knowing it.
- Refuse to store these keys on any electronic device, ever; otherwise, you're defeating the purpose of cold storage.
- Use a form of password protection known as BIP-38. This adds another layer of security, making the paper keys worthless without it.

Here's an example of how simple it is to create a paper wallet. You'll have it up and running in just a few minutes:

1. Use your browser and go to http://bitaddress.org
2. This will open the screen where your new public and private keys will be created.
3. The QR codes and private keys you are provided need not be saved; just click on the paper wallet.
4. Now you choose how many addresses you want to create.
5. Click the button to begin creating the amount of paper wallets you require.
6. Print out or store the paper wallets in a safe place offline.
7. If you choose not to print your wallets you should save them to a USB-based thumb drive in PDF format. The PDF file is a potential security breach, so you never want to save it on your hard drive (unless, of course, you plan to never again use this computer on the internet).
8. The QR code that appears on the left hand side must be scanned with your mobile bitcoin client. Alternatively you could send the public address to the Bitcoin client on your computer. Once this is completed you are ready to transfer bitcoin onto your wallet. The private key verifies ownership and means you can start spending! The private key can be scanned using the QR code.

In addition to the cold storage option, paper bitcoin wallets make a unique and useful gift, especially when you want to introduce a friend to the whole universe of cryptocurrency. A paper wallet is a delightful way to show your appreciation to a person who's helped you. Instead of a birthday gift card, you can give something unique: a paper Bitcoin wallet. A paper wallet can make a considerate wedding gift; in addition to the currency value, you are making it easier for the newlyweds to start their married life on a fresh financial footing.

Of course, your recipient will need their own wallet in order to transfer and use any bitcoin you give them. They will need to be willing to get involved in Bitcoin, but I'm sure you'd be willing to help them along, using your own newly acquired cryptocurrency skills.

Hardware Wallet

Another way to store your bitcoin away from the prying eyes of internet hackers and nasty viruses is to use a hardware wallet. You stash your wallet on an external hard drive, a thumb drive or another data storage device that can be unhooked from the internet.

This form of cold storage is very secure. You can now purchase cryptocurrency hardware wallets from $25 up to around $100. These dedicated wallets offer rock-solid security, offline private key generation and virus protection. They're also designed to be easy to use, making them the ideal solution for the newcomer to Bitcoin. The most popular hardware wallets are currently TREZOR, KeepKey and Ledger Nano S.

Mobile Wallet

Bitcoin wallets are not all that different from other software you've downloaded onto your phone; the same security measures apply. To spend bitcoin that are stored in your wallet, your private key is downloaded and installed on your phone. From a security point of view, you minimize the risk of your private key being picked up by others if it's isolated on your phone.

Mobile wallets are very convenient. Usually you will have your phone with you and that's all you'll need to access your Bitcoin wallet. A smart phone with internet access will let you perform bitcoin transactions as you move about.

The danger arises when your private key becomes vulnerable to unauthorized access. You'll want to back it up immediately after you have installed your chosen Bitcoin wallet. Regardless of which mobile wallet you choose, the software will contain a backup feature. You can also export a copy of your backup to cloud services or email it to yourself.

The most vital security measure is the authentication process. This is put in place to prevent funds from being misused or stolen off of your phone. Most mobile wallets come with an embedded PIN number. The PIN must be entered before the user can access the wallet, just as you would with a debit card. When the wrong PIN is entered a certain number of times, the wallet will lock and the instructions for how to unlock it will be sent via email or text to the owner. Or course, you'll want to set it up so a notification will be sent to an app *not* accessible by your phone!

Undoubtedly, when we talk about security and convenience, mobile wallets are your best bet, but the strength of your security depends entirely on you, the user. If you forget to back up your private key or if you leave your phone open for others to use, you are making yourself highly vulnerable to loss, whether by the permanent loss of the key or by the theft of an unsecured device and all its contents.

Bitcoin gives the user full responsibility and complete control, every step of the way; this is the reason people like Bitcoin, after all. Yet, the flip-side of this freedom means you're entirely responsible for its security. Protecting your cell phone wallet, while entirely up to you, is important enough that I would urge you to seriously consider the practical steps you can take to secure your wallets.

Web Wallet

Some companies offer wallet services for use with bitcoin. They serve as middlemen who will hold your coins and enable you to deposit and spend your bitcoin as you wish. Technically, the middleman takes away the hassle of security and administration for your account. However, this presents a single step away from the independent control that cryptocurrencies were established to bypass. Any wallet services company will require your personal information. Of course, this doesn't help at all if you are hoping to remain anonymous.

If you decide to go with the third party wallet provider, make sure you trust the company. I say this because, already in Bitcoin's brief history, we have seen Bitcoin holding companies disappear, go bust, or be hacked, leaving customers in the lurch with no way to get back their precious bitcoin.

Generally, you need to proceed with caution as the regulation side of Bitcoin is still under development in some areas of the world. I recommend you select a country with strong regulations already in place that are friendly to cryptocurrencies. As of this writing the Isle of Wight, the United Kingdom, and the United States are a few of the safest choices.

Online Wallet Security

Online Bitcoin wallets and banks have many similarities as they both handle the user's funds, plus users can send and receive funds and check their balance at any given time. When you deposit your money into your bank you expect and trust the bank to ensure that your money is safe, the same is unable to be said of Bitcoin. Since the beginning of Bitcoin, trust has been at the center and plays a huge part in its development.

While an online wallet service is really handy there are also major risks. Although storing bitcoin online and being able to access them from the browser seems advantageous you are relying solely on the wallet provider being honest.

When you choose to use an online wallet provider you are instructing them as a third party and they take full control of your funds. In this case, the main risk is that while you will know your online wallet address, you won't have access to the private key; in essence you've given up part of your control of your funds. If the wallet service you have chosen is then hacked or closed down, you lose all control you're your money that is stored in your wallet.

You also are fully responsible for keeping your wallet service account protected. Although most online providers offer additional security such as two factor authentication in most cases, no system is completely safe as they cannot stop your money from being taken if the service is hacked. If you absolutely must remain in full control of your funds at all times, then an online wallet is not for you. Online wallets do not provide you with full control and are not what Satoshi Nakamoto had in mind when he developed and launched Bitcoin.

Your Bitcoin Addresses

Your public address is similar to an email address as you can use it to send and receive digital information. Your addresses are case sensitive. If you mix up an address the funds will not transfer. Technically, you *can* keep using the same address again, but by creating a new address for each transaction you will give each transaction an additional layer of security.

Keeping Your Wallet Secure

You would never wander about with your wallet or purse on full display hanging from your handbag or back pocket, would you? Or keep the PIN for your bank card stuck to it? Obviously not. Well, the same security rules apply to your Bitcoin wallet.

Bitcoin Core has the capability to encrypt your password. This is advisable since it does give you added security and keeps your bitcoin as safe as possible.

Software Wallet

Software wallets are designed to add to a computer's hard drive. This is a highly secure way to hold your bitcoin, because the only way they can be accessed is from your computer. The software is fully supported, created and developed by Bitcoin and is referred to as Bitcoin Core.

Syncing Software Wallets

In order for your software wallet to have the latest information regarding your account you'll want to update or sync it regularly. Therefore, you must know the protocol to sync the program on your computer. When you install Bitcoin Core, the installation has to download all the transactions from the very first one. With this in mind, the download could take a few days to complete. It is important that you sync the software every time your computer has been shut down or the application has been closed; this will ensure that everything remains up to date.

Public And Private Keys

Your Bitcoin wallet is more than an address; it also is where your private and public keys for your Bitcoin addresses are held. Your private key consists of a random mixture of numbers and letters that are related mathematically to your Bitcoin wallet address. This key cannot be hacked, since it is governed by a highly encrypted algorithm.

You'll want to frequently back up your private key. Don't lose it; as I've already stated, there's no way to retrieve the information if it's destroyed. Already, there are thousands of bitcoin that cannot be accessed because the owners lost their keys or died without passing on the private key information.

You also have a public key. This is the cause of considerable confusion because most people mistakenly think their Bitcoin wallet's address is the same as their public key. Your wallet address is your public key, a code that has been scrambled to provide some security. Your address is 160 bits in length.

You use your public key as confirmation that you actually own the address and are opening it to send and receive funds. The public key is also based on a mathematical version of the private key. However, the relationship is so complicated that it would take millions of years for even the most powerful computer to crack it!

In addition to keys and the wallet address, your wallet also retains a log of all transactions, incoming and outgoing. Each transaction that is linked to your address is stored by your wallet so that you can see what you have spent and received at any given time. The wallet also stores the user preferences you have set up. The available preferences depend on the wallet type you are using and the platform you choose to serve as its host. Novice users will find life less complicated by using Bitcoin Core Client software. The preferences it offers are minimal, making it far easier to conquer the basic issues of handling your bitcoin.

Backup Systems

Now that you've created your wallet, the next step is to back it up. Your software will guide you through this process. You can back up your wallet using your hard drive or you can send it to a USB-based removable thumb drive. Because it will be encrypted, you do not have to worry should anything happen to your computer; your external backup will contain all the necessary information for you to continue using your bitcoin wallet.

Chapter 6: Understanding Bitcoin Transactions

Before you finish this chapter, you will understand Bitcoin transactions, you'll grasp the significance of network confirmations and have a solid understanding of Bitcoin fees. Bitcoin transactions basically consist of digitally transferring the ownership of a prearranged quantity of bitcoin. For example, if you own 20 bitcoin and you send 15 to user Sue, you are transferring those 15 bitcoin into Sue's wallet, leaving 5 remaining in your own wallet.

How Transactions Work

Simply put, a transaction begins when you communicate that you want to give a specific quantity of your bitcoin to another individual. For the transaction to be classed as valid, it must have at least one input. In Bitcoin, the word "input" refers to an "output" from an earlier transaction. When you spend bitcoin, you almost always get "change" back from your transaction. This change is the "output" of the transaction. Each input to a transaction will come from one or more outputs from previous transactions. Each input is digitally signed with the private key that belongs to the address initiating the bitcoin transfer.

If two or more inputs make up a single transaction, it purely means the bitcoin you send are coming from many different wallet addresses. For example, let's say you send 15 bitcoin to Sue with five of them coming from wallet number two, 4.75 bitcoin from wallet number five and the remaining from wallet number eight, it means that wallets one, three, four, six and seven have a zero balance and are unable to serve as an input, because no output is associated with those addresses.

Bitcoin transactions can also have multiple outputs. This indicates that a transaction has been split and sent to multiple addresses. For example, your wallet balance of 20 bitcoin will be sent to Sue (15 bitcoin) with the remaining 5 bitcoin sent to another wallet over which you have full control. This would be recorded on the blockchain as two separate outputs, one to Sue and the other to your other wallet address.

Bear in mind that cash payments and bitcoin payments are not all that different when it comes to transactions. The value of bitcoin associated with a combination of inputs will usually amount to more than the amount being sent and this yields a return in the form of change. When you make a cash transaction, your change is returned in the form of notes and coins. With bitcoin, your change arrives in the form of bitcoin that have returned to your bitcoin address. If a transaction's inputs total more than the transaction's outputs, the extra outputs would be returned to a unique address that was created to house the change.

There are several ways you can transfer bitcoin to someone else. First, you can request their bitcoin address and use the Bitcoin software installed on your device to perform the transaction. If you are a cell phone user, the transfer is easier; the donor scans the QR code that was generated by the recipient. All forms of Bitcoin software give the user the ability to create their own QR codes. These can display the wallet address where you want the funds to go, including the amount to be paid.

For example, we'll assume that over time your wallet has accrued 20 bitcoin, so you decide to send 15 bitcoin to Sue. This transaction has one input (the output you haven't spent from the transactions where you received the 20 bitcoin) and you then create two separate outputs. The first is the transaction in which you sent 15 bitcoin to Sue and the second is the "change", returning the extra five bitcoin to your wallet address.

Confirmations

Bitcoin confirmations are sent out once a transaction has been confirmed valid by the miners. Each block is deemed complete, along with all transactions that have taken place prior to yours. The transactions are then broadcast to all Bitcoin nodes and the nodes determine whether or not the transactions are complete and valid.

Each node on the Bitcoin network, once a valid transaction is broadcast, will provide a single network confirmation. A minimum of six confirmations are required for most transactions to be completed. Until the confirmations arrive, a transaction is considered in an in-between stage, hanging out between users. Only when the verification is lodged on the blockchain should you proceed. Before this point, security issues exist for all involved.

Don't be surprised if the time it takes for verification varies widely across transactions; this is perfectly normal. The majority of Bitcoin wallets will show a transaction as spent even if it has not reached the necessary six confirmations, since reaching the six may take an hour or more to achieve. A Bitcoin client cannot force confirmations, since this function is determined by the network. But, with Bitcoin block creation occurring at ten-minute intervals, if your pending transaction is broadcast and found by a network block before the new block is uncovered, the initial confirmation can happen quickly.

Any transaction with no confirmations is at risk for double spending. It is possible for users to initiate a second transaction for coins that are pending in a first transaction. Consequently, transactions with less than six confirmations are always risky. Because of this, payment processors and merchants are allowed to set the number of confirmations they require. For Bitcoin users who use Bitcoin software on their computer, these rules do not apply, because the funds will remain "unconfirmed" until all six confirmations are received. Mobile wallets, on the other hand, allow their users to spend any incoming funds much quicker.

Zero Confirmations

Generally, we say that transactions are irreversible. While this is true, almost every rule will have at least one exception. In this case, until the first confirmation has been received, it is possible to cancel a transaction. While the miners are in the process of putting together the next bitcoin block, you can back out. Since the process of mining a block takes around 10 minutes, you may have about that much time to change your mind about the transaction.

But don't count on it.

How Many Do You Need?

The number of confirmations required to complete a transaction depends on the requirements of the person you're paying. They base their requirements primarily on the monetary value of the transaction.

Generally, if the transaction is less than a thousand dollars, only one confirmation is necessary.

Up to $10,000, most exchanges will require only three confirmations. If your transaction involves a million dollars or more, the exchanges will require 60 confirmations. Most transactions, however, fall between there and ten thousand dollars, so they'll need only six confirmations.

Getting Six Confirmations

Remember, each confirmation will only occur with the introduction of a new block to the system network. This event occurs roughly each ten minutes. The block that contains your transaction provides the first confirmation. The remaining five confirmations can will take roughly an hour to appear. Only after all six transaction confirmations are in place for a transaction will the coins be available for further transactions.

This hour-long process can be a help or a hindrance. Waiting for more than six confirmations means the user has a far lower risk of falling prey to a double spend attack over the network. Remember, Bitcoin transactions are non-refundable, so if you accept a transaction that is lacking confirmations, you may be setting yourself up for financial disaster. It could take many hours until the network fully confirms a transaction. Delayed confirmations occur less frequently, however, now that we know the ten-minute hash rate in use to generate blocks on the network.

When the software receives the six confirmations, the transaction is "confirmed" for most practical uses. However, Bitcoin protocol doesn't stop there. Shortly after Bitcoin was originally launched, a piece of code was added to the Bitcoin protocol. This code stated that new coins (mined blocks) would only be considered valid when 100 confirmations had been received. Because of this, most Bitcoin mining pools will not reward miners until the transactions have received 120 confirmations.

Double Spending

While Bitcoin is extremely secure, there is always a weak point in any system. Bitcoin's Achille's heel has always been its vulnerability to double spending. Double spending occurs when a Bitcoin user has the ability to spend the same bitcoin twice. To attempt to prevent this from happening, the network verifies every single independent transaction. Consequently, while double spending is theoretically possible, it seldom occurs in real life.

When it comes to security no system is completely infallible, but Bitcoin protocol is a totally new form of technology, one that will take an enormous amount of computing power and intelligence to create a double spend. Double spends have occurred, but they are extremely rare and are usually identified and dealt with quickly. Where there's no need to know all the details, you should be aware of the five forms of double spending attacks that have emerged:

1. **Race** – Merchants and traders who accept unconfirmed payments are exposing themselves to a double spend if a fraudulent attempt successfully reports a transaction to the merchant but successfully duplicates the same coins in another transaction that manages to arrive first at the blockchain. The first transaction to arrive is accepted, while the slower one is rejected as invalid.

2. **Finney** – The Finney attack requires the assistance of a miner and takes place when a block is mined. The risk of this type of attack cannot be eliminated, no matter what precautions a merchant takes. The miner participates by following a specific sequence of events. This attack is major and expensive and would only make sense when the amount to be gained was vast.

3. **Vector76** – Also known as the one-confirmation attack, this form of double spending combines the race and the Finney attacks. In this attack a transaction with a single confirmation can be double spent. However, with Vector76 the same protection that was set in place against the race attack works well to significantly reduce the risk.

4. **Brute force** – This attack starts with a transaction being sent which then pays the merchant simultaneously to the blockchain fork being mined in private, with a double spend included instead. Once the confirmations reach the merchant, they send the goods. If the attacker gets lucky and finds more than the determined number of blocks, they release the fork and take back their coins.

Alternatively, the attacker can extend the fork and hope to catch up the network.

5. **50/51%** – If the attacker has control over half the network's hash rate, brute force would probably be 100% successful. This is because the attacker could create blocks far quicker than anyone else on the network. They can continue using this private fork until it eventually becomes longer than the branch constructed by the network.

Confirmation Zero

A trend is growing in the Bitcoin world that stems from merchants not waiting to obtain six confirmations to complete the Bitcoin payment. By not waiting, they have a far greater risk of falling victim to a double spend attack. It's extremely risky business to consider a payment completed without six network confirmations.

Regardless, it is up to the payment processors and merchants to decide how many confirmations they require before they validate a payment. Acting once the transaction has been made allows purchases to be completed, but it leaves merchants vulnerable to losing out on the sale in the long run.

Bitcoin Fees

Bitcoin is often described as a worldwide payment option with no transaction fee. This is true to a degree, but that's not quite the entire picture. The recipient of a Bitcoin transaction will not be charged, providing the transfer is from another user. However, sometimes a minimal fee is applied.

Most Bitcoin wallets will let you add a fee to your transactions if you wish. This is a common practice you can engage in when you want to speed transaction processing. If you include even a small transaction fee, your transaction will be favored over feeless transactions.

Transaction Speed

The priority of a transaction is determined by a complex mathematical formula. The calculated starts by dividing the age of the transaction by its size in bytes. The best weighted sum will be over 57,600,000. When there are more transactions pending than the current block can handle, any remaining transactions will need to wait for the next block, released ten minutes later.

Mining Fees

Bitcoin transactions are included into blocks by Bitcoin miners. By adding a transaction fee, you give a miner a little incentive to ensure that your transaction is included in their next block.

With no fees, miners have no incentive to confirm and validate the transactions. Although you are not obligated to include a fee, you will incentivize the miners when you do.

Multi-Signature Transactions

You may assume that full control of Bitcoin funds always remains with the end user; however, as the end user is the only person who knows the private key for the wallet, an even stronger form of security is now available. Having one user controlling their own wallet is fine, but matters are different when it comes to companies, friends or even family members who share a wallet. In this case, trust could become an issue.

If more than one user is involved in a project, it used to be a case of one user taking charge of the private key. However, if that user chooses to take the funds and run, everyone else is left in the lurch. As a result, Bitcoin has developed a multi-signature wallet, to ensure proper accountability across the shared ownership. With this kind of wallet, a private key is required from each of the wallet's owners before a transaction is considered properly authorized. .

Chapter 7: Blockchain Mysteries Revealed

This chapter will explain how blocks are used to unlock the blockchain's full potential By the time you've reached the end, you will have absorbed the key concepts of the blockchain and will understand how it functions within Bitcoin.

Blockchain – What Is It?

The blockchain is simply a public ledger that offers complete transparency to the Bitcoin system. It contains every Bitcoin transaction in its entirety since Bitcoin first began in 2009. All additional transactions are logged on the blockchain as they occur. The technology behind Bitcoin is easily capable of that much.

First, let's talk about what we mean by a block. If the blockchain were an accountant's ledger, it would be appropriate to view the original block as the ledger's first page.

Each new block on the network consists of a hash. A hash is a shorter, random mix of characters based on the previous block. Ever since the first block appeared on the network, a continuous chain of transactions have occurred, a block at a time. You can trace each transaction that occurs all the way back to the genesis of the initial block. Because each new page contains a summary of the previous pages, it makes sense that the ledger size will increase, extending the length of the blockchain as more data appear.

The Bitcoin blockchain consists of an open ledger. This ledger records each transaction as it occurs. Basically, the blockchain is a bookkeeping tool that provides complete transparency, with all transactions visible to the financial world. This total transparency is what traditional financial institutions fear. They don't want to lay out their numbers as openly as the blockchain.

Each node is a computer that runs the Bitcoin software. The software detects and validates new transactions. It also retains a copy of each transaction on the system. As transactions are added to the existing blockchain, the nodes retain a complete timeline of how Bitcoin has evolved financially.

Each new block is created in chronological order, containing the previous block's hash. If there's an inconsistency between a block and its predecessor, the network will reject the transaction as incorrect.

Blockchain Analytics

2014 saw a new trend emerging in Bitcoin's blockchain technology. Blockchain analysis arrived, adding a whole new market to the Bitcoin system. This analysis is only possible because of Bitcoin's transparency. Whether it is advantageous or harmful remains to be seen.

One thing that has assisted Bitcoin in its growth as a mainstream payment method, is being able to see how people are spending their bitcoin, not only by looking at the products and services bought and sold, but also by seeing how long they are holding the bitcoin they receive in their wallets. You can pay out bitcoin in the same way you spend your cash. You can make a bitcoin payment at any time, any place. Now that we can analyze how long people hold onto their coins, we can target our marketing to stimulate the rest of the population to use their bitcoin.

Blockchain analysis adds to the legitimacy of the whole platform. Because Bitcoin is so young, we are facing plenty of unknowns. Blockchain analysis helps us get a handle on some of those unknowns, making investment less of a leap in the dark. It provides valuable information to industry experts that will help Blockchain mature and continue to flourish.

Thanks to blockchain analysis, we can start to discern how bitcoin hoarding impacts the entire market. We can track trends that will tell us how people are spending their bitcoin and where most new wallets are coming from.

Understandably, a small proportion of the oldest bitcoin recorded on the network have not traded in years. Some may belong to the founder, Satoshi Nakamoto, but they may also belong to early investors who have now forgotten about Bitcoin completely. It could be possible that private keys have been lost, rendering funds held in those wallets completely useless. However, blockchain analysis can give us insight into the rate of unclaimable bitcoin.

Beyond Transactions

You can use the blockchain for more than you could ever imagine. You can track packages in real time, anywhere in the world. You can create copyright claims, fight online piracy and stop counterfeit products, just by using blockchain technology. Of course, the blockchain is used mostly for the financial side of things, to record transactions. Yet, I advise you to keep an open mind, remembering that blockchain technology is so much more than just a form of currency. The blockchain can go far beyond a financial transactions ledger. Here are some projects currently underway that prove how superbly blockchain technology can adapt to a variety of needs.

Decentralized storage: Users are given tokens for components of the blockchain that they allow to be stored on their device. Users can apply the tokens to store parts of their data on the blockchain, too. These are a few of the bona fide organizations involved in decentralized storage:
- Storj
- Maidsafe
- Nebulous
- Sia
- Filecoin

Extra blockchain layer - This adds an extra top layer to the blockchain that focuses on data storage, such as healthcare records. At the time of writing, some of the major players are:
- Factom
- Tieron
- Axoni
- E-bit
- Chain

The transparency of blockchain technology offers endless technological uses. Developers are only beginning to explore the extent of its potential.

Blockchain Applications

The current focus of blockchain developers is primarily financial services. This is understandable as Bitcoin is focused on combining financial services for everyone across the globe. However, vast unexplored areas exist.

The idea at the heart of blockchain applications are similar to Bitcoin, restoring all power to the user and eliminating the need for centralized companies and services. Because of the transparency provided by the blockchain, blockchain applications offer technological advances that are second to none.

Here is a sampling of the many ways blockchain-based applications can simplify your life:

- Lower your electric bills. The app compares multiple rates and switches services rapidly to take advantage of savings.
- Get deeper information about products. Blockchain-based information can provide details of where an item was manufactured and where the components came from. Developed by Provenance.
- Ride sharing vetted by the blockchain, without the middleman to take out a cut. Developed by Arcade City.
- Protect valuables with proof of ownership stored on blockchain.
- Ensure your charitable giving reaches the intended recipients. See BitGive.
- Check the source of your meat or produce. Developed by Provenance for the UK grocery market.
- Manage music royalties and ensure writers get paid for piece work. Apps developed by Smoogs and Revelator.
- Store your identification documents and information in a secure location. Certificates of birth, death, and marriage can be stored where authorized persons can access them.

  You can control what information you reveal to which people. If you want to buy cigarettes, for example, the clerk only needs to see proof that you are of age, so that's the extent of the information you provide, nothing else.

- Store your will in a secure location accessible by your attorney or executor upon your death. See MyWish.

Become A Developer

Blockchain's technology is a unique development. There's nothing else like it in the world, so you can count on a pretty steep learning curve at the start. However, any blockchain-related skills you can gain will be highly marketable in the foreseeable future. If you can learn to create blockchain applications, you'll most likely be in demand for a long time.

It can be very time-consuming to create and develop a blockchain-based application. There is a huge amount of code to be written and multiple outcomes to account for. These applications require a substantial amount of funding. Yet, venture capitalist investment continues to rise, regardless of bitcoin's volatile ups and downs.

The blockchain is all about creating communities that make choices more accessible to the average person. Much of the time, a group of people with the same idea will work together and share ways to improve it. The obvious example is the number of alternative digital currencies that have arisen since Bitcoin appeared on the scene. This results in the developing blockchain not being tied to one program. One of blockchain developers' greatest assets is diversification. Only time will reveal whether this community-styled spirit will continue or if the process will become commercialized.

Bitcoin 2.0

For several services, ranging from capital controlling to investment vehicles and all things in between, Bitcoin has been considered a currency. However, people have started to realize that Bitcoin is far more than a payment method. Bitcoin 2.0 provides an application and a platform that reflects that reality.

Bitcoin and blockchain technology will be pivotal in providing further enhancements to the financial world. The financial sector has seen little to no change over the last 45 years, so I'd imagine ample opportunity remains for improving on the status quo.

Blockchains provide a perfect replacement for authentication processing on sites such as Twitter or Facebook. The potential has not gone unnoticed; many financial institutions are now looking into ways to use the blockchain in their businesses. Admittedly, even though some of these businesses can't see a future for Bitcoin in currency terms, they do want to make use of the blockchain, because it offers almost unlimited potential for applications that will provide real-world improvements.

Bitcoin 2.0 is attracting plenty of attention, because it can broadcast blocks of data on the network. Instead of including information about transactions, Bitcoin blocks are able to transfer data of any kind to users and accomplish this openly. Engineers and developers are currently looking into the possibilities of using this technology to manage and store copyright claims, passport photos, real estate registrations and other information.

Bitcoin 2.0 will vastly improve the current Bitcoin exchange. To this date, the majority of exchanges allow Bitcoin users to send, receive and store digital currency. Bitcoin 2.0 will introduce additional features like peer-to-peer lending, accounts that yield interest and quite possibly the capacity to lend financial security without any assistance from a broker or bank.

Bitcoin 2.0 will also do away with the middleman when it comes to buying and selling. Technically, ownership of products could be tied to digital tokens, which can then be transferred to another blockchain user, together with a payment for the transaction. Realistically, there is vast potential for e-commerce transactions around the world to take place on the blockchain.

Another option for Bitcoin 2.0 employs blockchain technology to provide virtual identification cards that users can implement to complete verification processes. Instead of having to send sensitive information to third parties, who would then store them on a central server, the virtual ID card could be verified by the blockchain. This means the person who owns the identity card has total control of the data, while the seller is unable to store any of the information.

Bitcoin 2.0 is set to create a new type of decentralized market in the future since it becomes a new branch of innovative technology under current construction. However, let's not move away from the idea that blockchain technology relies on the support of the community for its existence. The main purpose of Bitcoin 2.0 is to create a decentralized service with applications that will encourage people to start their own businesses in whatever line of work they wish to pursue. It is only my opinion, but I feel there is little that Bitcoin 2.0 will not achieve, once it becomes a part of mainstream life.

Chapter 8: Mining Bitcoin

This chapter will dig right into what mining is and how it works, providing a complete understanding of cloud mining and explain what it takes to set up a mining operation.

Today, mining is not a possibility for most individuals. No longer are you able to use the existing components of your personal computer to mine bitcoin. Today, the cost of essential hardware alone is beyond the reach of the average person. Add to that the electricity needed to power this energy hog and run the banks of fans necessary to cool the equipment and you have a figure that begins at around half a million dollars. Right now, mining is only truly workable in China, where low electricity costs would allow a mining operation to see some profit.

Now, let's explore what is involved in mining for bitcoin.

Mining

The process known as bitcoin mining centers around creating more bitcoin, up until the twenty-one-million-coin cap is reached. Bitcoin are not issued by the government or banks and they do not magically appear. No, they are created by people and machines solving math equations, the miners.

Without bitcoin miners, there would be no new bitcoin in circulation. Although this would not be a problem for most people, it does mean that no further transactions would be confirmed by the Bitcoin network and this in itself is far more concerning. If no blocks could be built on the Bitcoin network, all transactions would cease and pending transactions would be left hanging, dormant and unconfirmed and the entire operation would grind to a halt.

Bitcoin mining is not just about creating new bitcoin; it is also a process that adds recorded transactions to the blockchain. Each transaction made using bitcoin must be recorded in a data block, the "ore" block miners are working to discover. As soon as a transaction becomes included in a Bitcoin block it gains one confirmation from the network.

As more people compete against one another to mine a block, the complexity level of the math equations steadily rises. Using a formula where the blocks newly mined remain constant, one block is mined every ten-minutes. Knowing this, we can calculate when the very last block will be mined, in the year 2140.

Mining from home has become almost impossible unless you are fortunate enough to live where you can use either free or hugely subsidized electricity. Today the majority of Bitcoin miners are located in China, where electricity is cheapest.

Let's Go Down To The Mine!

Mining exists to build up a system of Bitcoin nodes that allow multiple locations where a broadcast transaction can be tested and certified as valid. For a transaction to be officially spendable it needs to have six confirmations on the network.

When Bitcoin first started, each block a user mined was rewarded with fifty bitcoin. When 210,000 bitcoin were reached, the value of a mined bitcoin was cut in half. As of this writing, the block reward stands at 12.5 bitcoin and it is expected to halve again in 2020. This means that bitcoin miners are receiving less and less for each block they mine. As a result, the fees you attach to your transactions are expected to become increasingly valuable as time goes on.

You pay the miner for including your transaction in a block scheduled to be mined. While most of a miner's money is currently made from block rewards, transaction fees are expected to play a much greater role in future earnings.

The ecosystem of Bitcoin has dramatically changed since its inception; it now requires specialist hardware to have any chance of being profitable. It was inevitable that the high costs of mining would become an issue eventually; because of this, mining pools came into existence. Today individual miners have largely disappeared, replaced by huge mining pools. With the power of these massive computers, the odds of locating the next block are increased greatly and the proceeds are then split among the individual participants according to the amount of computer power they provided.

Understanding Mining

Unlike governments that can print more currency as needed, Bitcoin has a limited quantity of coins. As I stated earlier, the cap, set at twenty-one million bitcoin, will be reached by 2140. Until then, miners will continue to use their specialized computer programs to mine the Bitcoin network.

Once transactions appear on the network, miners pick them up and form them into a Bitcoin block. The Bitcoin block then goes through the process of verification and after being thoroughly vetted, all the transactions that have created it are logged within the blockchain. For each new block formed on the network, an additional network confirmation appears.

The miners play an essential role to ensure that the blockchain is correct and its integrity remains intact while recording the information from the Bitcoin block. Following this, a complicated math formula is applied to the Bitcoin data block, changing it into an entirely new one.

This new and different block is made up of a shorter, random set of numbers and letters we call a "hash." Bitcoin miners can solve these hashed values far easier than a complete data block because these new blocks are created and mined on average ten minutes and these hashes together require miners to solve a far more complicated formula. The more complex the equations become, the more expensive grow the hardware components needed to process them

After the hash has been resolved, it is stored on the blockchain along with the original block. This process verifies every transaction contained within the block, labeling each transaction within it with one network confirmation. While hashes are easier for miners to solve than blocks, the ever-increasing difficulty balances things out to keep blocks appearing steadily, ten minutes apart.

The system utilizes hashes because they are stable and cannot be corrupted. They're the perfect way to seal the confirmation portion of the process. Each hash linked to the previous block is valid, as well as those blocks coming after it.

It is impossible to count the many companies, individuals and hardware manufacturers involved in this process, because of the highly specialized hardware in use. There is fierce competition, but the bitcoin reward remains attractive to miners worldwide. Although the difficulty of mining has increased dramatically, so has the network's computing power, strengthening the network. Larger mining operations now have a far more significant possibility of discovering the next block and earning rewards based on their input. Mining operations are responsible for increasing the strength and security of the entire Bitcoin network.

Mining In The Cloud

As we have explained, mining with home-based computers is almost impossible for the majority of people, because of electrical loads, specialized cooling equipment and hardware maintenance costs. Consequently, some companies rent their own mining hardware out; this is referred to as cloud mining.

Although this sounds like the perfect solution for those wishing to invest in Bitcoin at this present moment, you'll want to weigh the advantages against the disadvantages before you commit to using this service. The greatest potential danger is that not all cloud mining facilities are legitimate. As with any virtual market, cloud mining has its share of shysters, Ponzi schemers and other illegal players.

The profitability of cloud mining depends on the current price of the Bitcoin. To make a profit, a Bitcoin price of $300 to $350 is needed, based the Bitcoin rate at this writing.

Cloud Mining Advantages

When it comes to Bitcoin, you need money to create more money. It is impossible to get into mining without some upfront investment. However, cloud mining lets you participate in mining without buying the ultra-expensive hardware.

When you sign up for cloud mining you are in essence renting the hardware from a third party who purchased, installed and got the mining operation up and running. Neither are you paying for any of the necessary shipping fees. This will dramatically reduce your startup costs.

An investment is still needed when you sign up for cloud-based mining services. Most of these organization will offer either annual or lifetime contracts, during which time the company agrees to mine bitcoin for you. Obviously, this comes at a cost, which varies by the provider. As their customer, you will be cloud mining bitcoin from the moment you both have signed the contract. You will begin to receive earnings and you will find your initial investment returned at either a slow and steady rate or almost immediately. Unfortunately, one can never tell exactly how much you'll receive; your return is based on current market value.

Bitcoin cloud mining currently looks like a relatively safe option for those wanting to participate in mining activities. However, as with any type of investment, it may take time before the profits start to roll in, so plan to be patient. The amount of return depends on a host of factors, including the current price of bitcoin, the difficulty of mining and the computer power received by the Bitcoin network.

Cloud Mining Disadvantages

As a cloud mining customer, you will never have full control over the hardware you are renting; you'll never physically access the mining equipment. You are putting your trust in a third party to provide what you have signed up for and to honestly track and remit your share of earnings.

The profit payments are the primary focus of most issues surrounding cloud mining. There are many reasons you may think your payments are short. Rising electricity costs, unexpected hardware maintenance charges, suppliers raising prices and the changing value of the Bitcoin are all legitimate items that can eat into your profits.

Because cloud mining involves dependence on a service provider you are actually going against Bitcoin's underlying philosophy. You're yielding partial control of your finances to someone outside of yourself.

When you get involved in cloud mining, you become responsible for electrical and equipment maintenance charges. Even though you don't own the hardware, you're using electricity and causing wear and tear to the equipment, so these costs are passed onto you.

If you care about the environment, consider the carbon emissions impact of the mining operation you contract with. While many European countries now get their electricity primarily from renewable energy sources, China, a major mining locale, is one of the world's largest users of fossil fuels.

One major misunderstanding people have regarding cloud mining is to assume they are buying a specified quantity of computer power and that the rewards they receive have a direct correlation to how much power was used. In reality, it doesn't work this way. With the variable maintenance and computer operation costs factored in, there is not a reliable one-to-one correspondence.

Smart investors can still turn a profit from cloud mining, provided that they have done their own research and calculated a viable plan for success.

Risks Of Cloud Mining

Probably the greatest risk of cloud mining is the bogus service provider. Most cloud mining services will provide photographs of their mining spaces; however, it's all too easy to pass off a fake photo.

It's rare for a cloud mining service to be hacked, but when it is, customers earnings are bound to be affected. User investments can go missing, forcing a service provider to reduce earnings to recoup the losses.

As of this writing, there are a handful of confirmed-legitimate cloud mining services in operation. Each one has its strengths and weaknesses, so you'll need to do your own homework before you commit. Don't just dive in because it's on this list. That said, here are the cloud miners that made the cut as of this writing:

- Hashflare
- Genesis Mining
- Via BTC
- Nicehash
- Hashing24
- Eobot

If you decide to buy a cloud mining contract, you need to remember that something superior could be just around the corner. Bitcoin cloud mining is changing, adjusting and evolving to become more competitive every day. It's vital that you research the current situation for yourself, so you can be sure that your well-informed decision is based on current data.

Bitcoin Mining Made Secure

The Bitcoin network will only ever be secure and strong thanks to people supporting it, whether by dedicating computer power or running a Bitcoin node. One of the greatest threats to the Bitcoin network is a 51% attack, but additional computer power reduces any chance of malicious attackers being able to gain majority control of the network and bringing Bitcoin to its knees.

Miners become miners because of the money they hope to gain. Some individuals devote themselves to mining simply to improve network security; they consider the money as a bonus.

Wherever you stand, mining secures the network through the confirmation of transactions and by extending the blockchain. Mining protects the network and sustains it as a distributed neutral financial platform. The more miners we have, the greater power we have to prevent a biased system. If anyone comes by enough computing power to control a major amount of the platform, they still can only confirm their own network blocks, leaving plenty of other transactions for other people to hash.

Bitcoin mining is incredibly resource-intensive and is set to become even moreso as time goes on. Each individual block on the network requires further confirmation by other Bitcoin nodes. Once the nodes receive and verify that there has been no tampering, the new coins are released and their payment is the motivation that the miners require to continue pointing all their resources at Bitcoin. With greater resources the network gains higher-levels of security and the cycle begins all over again.

Running a Mine

As I've stated, it's harder than ever before to get involved in Bitcoin mining. The hardware required is constantly increasing in power and complexity, meaning more cost to the miner. However, there are still ways you can get involved. You just need plenty of resources (read, *money*).

The Hardware

When Bitcoin started up, back in 2009, the mining process was simple. Users just had to install the Bitcoin client software on their computer, synchronize it with the network and ensure that the checkbox was selected in the mining tab. Any computer, even a laptop, could be used to mine, because competition was sparse and the number crunching required was fairly simple.

Gradually, the calculations became more complex and starting demanding more processing power. Bitcoin enthusiasts discovered that their gaming graphics cards, designed for number crunching, could handle the mining process more handily. Soon they were off and running again, at faster speeds than ever.

Then came the Field Programming Gate Array (FPGA). The FPGA has the ability to produce computation power similar to that produced by the graphics cards, but to process items much more efficiently. By 2013, the FPGA was standard mining equipment.

Bitcoin ASIC became available shortly thereafter, dramatically reducing the electricity consumption while substantially out-performing other mining products. However, the noise made by the new processer meant you no longer could sleep in the same room with the machine. Plus, although the system came with its own built-in cooling device, temperatures could still exceed 150°F. The device is also huge and heavy, meaning more costs for transporting it. The hardware has now grown so large that we're swiftly outgrowing the house.

ASICs can't process any faster than 1.5 terrahash, so to keep up with the burgeoning competition, you'll need to use massive amounts of these processors. The concept of cloud mining is sounding more attractive, now that it takes a large building to house the processing arrays and their attendant cooling equipment.

Working Out Your Costs

Whether you sign up for a cloud mining contract or buy your own hardware, it is essential to work out your initial costs, projected earnings and timeline to profitability. The cost of Bitcoin mining goes beyond your investment into the hardware, logistical costs and import fees. You'll need to calculate your projected power usage and determine how much this will cost. All you can do is check your electric rates, work out the price per kilowatt hour, then calculate the amount of electricity your mining hardware will use on a daily basis.

Compare your total to the income you stand to make in a day. Of course, your income will depend heavily on the market value of Bitcoin, which fluctuates frequently.

In addition to the cost of equipment and electricity, you'll need to factor in projected maintenance and repair costs, including lost profits during down times. Since ASIC miners don't all include a power supply, you may need to purchase your own, so be careful to include this if required.

You'll also want to calculate the value of the time you invest and the effort you put into getting things going as well as keeping them humming along. Most manufacturers release firmware for mining hardware regularly and fix any glitches regularly, to ensure the hardware is consistently functioning at maximum capacity.

Profitability Calculator

To simplify matters, you'll find several sites online that specialize in producing accurate mining profit calculations. All you must do is enter your electricity cost along with certain details regarding your hardware. These sites can also provide reasonably accurate predictions for the not-so-distant future.

Chapter 9: Doing Business With Bitcoin

Buying and spending bitcoin is attractive enough when you understand exactly how it works. However if you own a business, a world of opportunities open up. Read on, as I am going to explain how you can incorporate bitcoin into your current business structure. This chapter will show you how to welcome bitcoin into your business model and attract a host of bitcoin users who are on the lookout for fresh opportunities.

Why Choose Bitcoin?

In brief, because this emerging form of digital currency, by its very design, eliminates many of the challenges faced by most businesses today. Bitcoin is a much more secure transaction base than credit cards and it's cheaper to use. Whether you're a retailer or a wholesaler, whether you run an internet-based storefront or an actual physical shop, bitcoin can eliminate many of the hassles related to sales transactions.

No More Chargebacks

If you have ever accepted credit card payments, you will understand how frustrating chargebacks can be. In addition, even if you are 100% certain the card owner is the person who made the purchase, the fee you pay the company for processing the transaction continues to rankle. On top of that, any time a charge is rejected, you suffer insult added to injury when the card provider penalizes you with processing fees for a fraudulent payment, especially after you've already shipped out the goods!

What would you think if I told you bitcoin can prevent this from ever happening to you again? As I explained in previous chapters, when a Bitcoin transaction is initiated, it is vetted by the entire network. You can watch the confirmations come in before you choose to complete the transaction.

Bitcoin payments are irreversible once they have received their first confirmation. After someone pays you they cannot snatch the payment away from you the minute the order is complete. With Bitcoin there are no chargebacks

Once a Bitcoin transaction is completed, it cannot be cancelled or reversed. The system can't even process a chargeback if it wanted to! Customers have no power to initiate this process themselves. If you really need to refund the customer, *you'll* be the one to initiate the new transaction.

Super-low Transaction Fees

It's almost impossible to do business today without accepting card payments. However, the fees are so high that it's expensive for small firms to process credit cards; it cuts too deeply into their profits.

Here's another instance where bitcoin can help. Frankly, this is often the main reason many organizations choose to accept bitcoin.

On average, credit card transactions charge two to four percent, with additional fees on top. This may not seem much, but if you are giving up four percent of each sale it will add up to a significant chunk of your profit. By comparison, bitcoin usage can slash these rates to less than one percent. In this way, bitcoin instantly adds up to five percent to your revenue, just by choosing to use it over credit cards.

Faster Payment For Large Purchases

Large international transactions may need considerable time to process. It is natural to have to wait for over a week for an international wire confirmation to deposit into your account. Each time you repeat this procedure it can feel like it takes forever.

Once again, Bitcoin provides the solution by eliminating the long wait. Regardless of payment size or its destination, your transaction will provide the first confirmation in just a few minutes. Of course, you'll want to watch for several transactions if this is your first transaction with the customer, but this will require only a matter of minutes, not the days of waiting you would experience otherwise.

This breakthrough is massively advantageous for small businesses; many avoid international transactions altogether, because of the transaction fees and other problems associated with them. This invisible barrier is entirely eradicated by bitcoin.

Transparent Historical Transactions

No one wants to dig through mountains of paperwork to track their business transactions. Honestly, no one relishes complicated bookwork that makes it difficult to track down multiple transactions from all their sources.

Bitcoin maintains records of each transaction you make, vastly simplifying your own record-keeping. Everything is out in the open, displayed for all to see. Even if you're worried about privacy this is no problem, because your wallet address doesn't specifically identify you.

Accepting Bitcoin

By now you should understand why accepting Bitcoin payments is a great idea. So, let's look at how you can set yourself up to do this yourself. It is not as hard as you might think. Plenty of people are working hard to simplify the process; after all everyone wants to be the frontrunner in Bitcoin merchant technology. It's time to evaluate some of the best payment processors available at this writing.

Processing Payments

There are two payment processors that stand out from the rest of the crowd: CoinBase and BitPay. It is worth looking at both, to have an informed decision about which would best fit the needs of your business.

CoinBase

One of the most well-known Bitcoin payment processors worldwide is CoinBase. It is massive and handles millions of transactions every day. It is poised to become the number one service provider for business owners.

CoinBase has made it simple to exchange Bitcoin for any other form of currency. When you begin to handle Bitcoin payments, CoinBase will automatically convert the incoming funds to your local currency. At close of business, the funds are transferred into your business checking or savings account. There is a three-day processing delay, but this is still better than many traditional credit card processors.

Better yet, for many businesses, the processing is free. CoinBase costs nothing until you have amassed a million dollars in transactions. After that point, CoinBase charges a flat fee of 1%. It will take a while for most businesses to cross this threshold, but even so, they will still save plenty of money over other methods of payment.

What makes CoinBase stand out above its competitors is its refund platform. Bitcoin payments are non-refundable which means that you need to calculate and send manual refunds. CoinBase's new platform allows you to refund transactions as easily as you can payments that have been made by credit cards.

BitPay

Coming in a close second behind CoinBase is BitPay. BitPay was one of the first payment processors to come on the market and it has seen steady growth ever since.

This platform makes it simple for people to pay you in bitcoin by offering multiple options. Customers can scan a QR code, they can copy and paste a wallet address, or they can click on a link to pay directly using Bitcoin software. Regardless of a person's experience – or lack of it – with Bitcoin, your customers will find it easy to pay for their purchases in bitcoin, ensuring that the money lands in your wallet.

From your point of view things could not be easier. Most shopping cart systems can easily adapt to a bitcoin platform. Whether you are operating from a brick and mortar location or an online business site, the process is uncomplicated. For websites, it requires a simple line of code to add Bitcoin to your options for processing incoming payments. Brick and mortar stores can take advantage of an app that accepts payments, or they can use an application that integrates with their existing system.

BitPay has one benefit over CoinBase. Bitcoin payments are converted into your currency and go directly into your specified bank account.

You'll be able to access the funds the following day. This is especially valuable when you are dealing with multiple suppliers who require rapid repayment. Bitpay's 24-hour turnaround gives it a solid advantage over credit card processors, which can take a week or longer to release funds for your use.

The conversion system is included with a free package, offered to get businesses set up for receiving payments in bitcoin. Free is far cheaper than the cost of getting set up to receive credit card payments. Since these services don't require any added infrastructure, you will find it simple to implement.

BitPay is so easily implemented that you will quickly go from zero knowledge to Bitcoin expert. The free service will serve you well and if your business grows beyond the scope of the free service, you will find a variety of paid plans that still save you money over credit card processing. The paid plans include VPN access, QuickBooks and other valuable features that will become increasingly helpful as your business grows. If your business is already well established, you may find it beneficial to start out with a paid plan.

Online Stores

Online stores were the first to begin accepting bitcoin, but now anyone can join the revolution. You'll find plenty of processors available and these companies have streamlined the setup process as much as possible. You'll even notice most e-commerce sites are now able to integrate bitcoin payment gateways.

Brick And Mortar Stores

Brick and mortar stores may be the only thing that is easier than taking bitcoin on your website. If you already use a point of sale system, it is quick and easy to add bitcoin as a payment option. Before you know it, you'll be ready to accept bitcoin as a method of payment.

If you are using an older point of sale system, you may need to upgrade, or at least rethink how you can incorporate bitcoin payment processing as part of your business model. While it's possible to process bitcoin payments without a payment processer, you will probably find the bookkeeping a major hassle without it. Yes, there will be a bit of a learning curve, but once you're up and running and customers start using bitcoin to pay for their purchases, you'll likely be pleased with the results.

Chapter 10: Keeping It Legal

It's time to look at taxation and its impact on your bitcoin. We'll increase your understanding of the regulations surrounding bitcoin and talk about the ideas that surround licensing.

Anything we don't understand can appear frightening. It's natural to want to control our world, whether we're talking about childhood monsters under the bed or tax officials looming large in adult life. Even though it would feel good to be in control, Bitcoin is only partially "controllable." It won't help us to ban Bitcoin from our lives, especially if we're in business; it is developing into a staple of commerce.

Why would we want Bitcoin banned? Even though the platform is in constant flux and massive question marks surround this unique form of buying and selling, it appears to be gaining a toehold in our world. Yes, there are numerous aspects of Bitcoin that do need to be investigated further, in order to build a sensible regulatory framework. It's perfectly legal to pay for your purchases using Bitcoin. Even though banks have broadcast warnings about the risks associated with bitcoin usage, it cannot be all *that* bad, since they have seen no need to outright ban it.

The government and other legal authorities are worried because Bitcoin is not controlled by one central figure. Bitcoin is every bit a true democracy: everyone who uses Bitcoin helps to determine its future. Decentralization is a completely new technological process that people really don't understand. This in itself is enough to scare anyone who is accustomed to relying on Important People in Charge. In a society that has been trained to trust powerful authority figures, people tend to derive their sense of safety from accountability. Bitcoin, by giving individuals the responsibility for overseeing their own transactions, is setting the world on its ear. Of course, anything *that* new and different can easily appear as just another monster under the bed.

Let's examine how the legalities of Bitcoin look in different nations. While opinions and policies are rapidly shifting – and they'll continue to wobble all over the place for a while – this general summary will give you a feel for what you can expect to experience as you expand your bitcoin transactions into other corners of the globe. The major issues we'll tackle pertain to regulation and legality.

Taxation

Regardless of the warnings governments and central banks have issued about Bitcoin, most countries want to adopt this digital currency for a simple reason: they can tax it.

Digital currency can be used to pay wages or as a form of income and because of this it can be taxed. Choosing to use Bitcoin to pay for services and goods is also taxable in some countries. Since governments are likely to reap huge benefits from this new source of monetary transactions, they are slightly hesitant to put up any opposition to its use.

Wherever you do business, you'll be advised to keep up to date on the tax laws because they shift more often than the desert sand. I would advise you to check with your own government to see how you can use Bitcoin and to learn what – if any – taxes will apply to your bitcoin transactions.

Taxation guides have already been produced in Bulgaria, Brazil, Canada, Denmark and Finland for how Bitcoin can be used, although some are not in effect as yet. On the other hand, New Zealand, Belgium, Hong Kong, Greece and Japan have announced that they have no plans to tax digital currencies at this point.

Obviously, each country is looking at Bitcoin and the impact it is wielding on its economy. Because of the global nature of bitcoin transactions and the platform's decentralization, some regulations will need to be agreed upon globally before individual countries will be able to tackle the issues of regulation and taxation. The primary item at issue now, is whether Bitcoin is considered a form of currency, or whether it should be considered a kind of property.

Many countries already have laws on the books to block terrorism financing and to cover the laundering of money. These regulation often reside under the label of the Financial Action Task Force, or FATF. However, some governmental actions will required on the part of many countries, before regulations and tax guidelines for Bitcoin can be agreed upon. Setting this aside, the lure of regulating and apply taxes to bitcoin – and what bitcoin purchases – could certainly stimulate countries to work together, in the interest of laying the groundwork for a solution that everybody can apply.

Pro-Bitcoin Countries

Each country handles taxation differently. In addition they change their rules frequently, making it impossible for this part of the book to remain current for long. However, I will give you the best information that is currently available as of this writing. This will at least give you a general idea where the various nations stand with regards to cryptocurrencies and how to regulate them.

In Europe, the EU is the main decision-maker. But some countries have produced their own tax guidelines for Bitcoin. At this time, the European Union has come to no clear decision on Bitcoin and tax regulations.

While Asia as a whole is quiet and undecided, Singapore taxes Bitcoin as an asset or property. Because it's viewed as a type of good in Singapore, bitcoin is subject to a value-added tax (VAT) or a sales tax when individuals buy or sell using bitcoin.

As things stand right now, around 30% of the countries in the world accept bitcoin as legal. Less than four percent of countries have declared it illegal. That leaves the remaining majority of the governing bodies in the world uncommitted to either position. In many of these countries, even some where cryptocurrencies have been officially banned, bitcoin are traded anyhow. This entity is so new that most governments have not yet gotten around to deciding what they want to do about it. Consequently, there's nothing to prevent people from opening up exchanges and trading bitcoin freely all over the world.

Here's a brief snapshot of some of the crypto-players at the moment, along with any current indication we have that shows how they are handling taxation:

- **Australia** – The government of Australia considers bitcoin a form of currency and applies a Goods and Services tax (GST) to any bitcoin transaction in excess of AUD$10,000.
- **Belarus**–This country has legalized cryptocurrencies. Recently, the president announced that Bitcoin and its ilk will remain exempt from capital gains taxes until 2023.
- **Belgium** –Belgium has declared Bitcoin exempt from value-added tax.
- **Brazil** – The Receita Federal, more often referred to as the tax authority of Brazil, has issued the following tax guidance for Bitcoin. Digital/Virtual currencies are considered assets and are assessed a 15% capital gains tax when a sale is completed. However, they have decided this tax will apply only to bitcoin transactions that exceed R$35,000. Anyone holding more than this amount must declare it correctly at year's end.
- **Bulgaria** –Bulgaria is among the few countries in Europe that has absorbed bitcoin into its existing tax regulations. The National Reserve Agency considers the sale of any type of digital currency a form of income. Because of this, a tax of 10% has been imposed.
- **Canada** – In Canada, bitcoin that are used for buying and or selling goods or services fall under a barter category, where any profits from these commodities are viewed as capital or income.

Each bitcoin is looked at individually and any profits are taxed via an owner's inventory at year's end. Assuming that these are business-related transactions, these are included with a person's taxable income.
- **Denmark** – Denmark is moving toward an entirely cashless economy, so it makes sense that it would be pro-Bitcoin. This country does not tax your bitcoin transactions and you don't pay capital gains tax, either.
- **European Union (EU)** – Bitcoin has been deemed a currency here. Consequently, at this point, value-added taxes (VAT) do not apply, but sales taxes do.
- **Finland** – In this country Bitcoin is a commodity. It is exempt from value-added tax. Finland took their own stance on Bitcoin in 2014. Bitcoin, the product of mining, was classed as income, so it's taxed as a capital gain. However, because the government

doesn't acknowledge Bitcoin as acceptable currency, it is classed as a commodity. If you're confused about this scenario, so is everyone else. The government is currently studying how they can create a workable tax system for cryptocurrencies.

- **Germany** – Germany has always been viewed as a forward thinking country with regards to bitcoin taxation. If you hold your bitcoin longer than a year they are no longer subject to capital gains tax, which at present time stands at 25%. Germany considers Bitcoin currency as "private money."
- **Isle of Man** – is self-governing and quite surprisingly is one of a few locations with an intelligent strategy in place for digital currencies. The exchanges in this country need to obey strong rules that include knowing and identifying customers, combatting terrorist finance and preventing the laundering of money.

Unlike most other countries globally, the Isle of Man is proactive regarding Bitcoin and other digital currencies; it has already taken steps toward creating its own regulatory framework. Currently, cryptocurrencies including bitcoin do not fall under the auspices of FSA-licensed activities. However, the companies are obliged to operate within the laws that make up the 2008 Proceeds of Crime Act. Therefore, they have already taken a sensible stance that requires new users to register, but waives the many licensing regulations normally insisted upon by the FSA.

Because of this, a true entrepreneurial spirit thrives on the island. The Isle of Man has seen cryptocurrency flourish there. While regulations will likely be phased in over time, this stance should help legitimize Bitcoin in the long run.

- **Malta** – One of the most supportive nations for cryptocurrencies, this island nation offers exemption from capital gains taxes to foreigners in the country. It welcomes bitcoin and some of the most extensive exchanges in the world are located here.
- **Netherlands** – Matters of bitcoin and crypto-taxation are very straightforward in the Netherlands. Bitcoin is viewed as just another currency is and taxed accordingly.
- **Nigeria** – The nation prosecuted its first case of cryptocurrency fraud in 2017. While the government has not banned bitcoin, it is

not considered legal tender and warnings have been issued against the dangers of fraud that may occur.

- **Slovenia** – Slovenia made the decision to levy no tax on sales of bitcoin made to exchanges or other users. However, Bitcoin is taxed as an income similarly to regular currency, with the tax determined by the exchange rate at the time of its levy.
- **South Africa** – Bitcoin is growing in popularity in this area. While the government doesn't acknowledge it as legal tender (nor any other form of cryptocurrency), it expects you to pay capital gains taxes on anything you earn. They are still deliberating, however, on what to do about value-added taxation.
- **United Kingdom** – Currently the UK treats digital currency beyond the scope of value-added tax, which is very welcomed by the business sector.
-

Yet Jersey, a dependent of the British Crown, has suddenly decided to regulate Bitcoin. Details are pending.

- **United States** – The USA is still pondering if it will tax Bitcoin and if so. how this will be accomplished. As the impact to the economy is still unknown, determining the right percentage for tax is difficult. It is also struggling to determine which people and which businesses would fall under what taxable categories.

At this point, the IRS considers bitcoin a form of property, not a type of currency. If the government were to reverse this position, Bitcoin income could conceivably become subject to any of one to three possible categories: hobby income, gambling income, or wages. Just to complicate things further, each category is taxed at a different percentage!

The US Treasury considers Bitcoin as a money services business, not as a form of currency. This means exchanges and other bitcoin processing agencies are expected to follow the reporting guidelines spelled out in the Bank Secrecy Act.

You can't avoid taxes by using Bitcoin or other virtual currencies. You'll be wise to avoid even the appearance of tax evasion while all these issues are being thrashed out. Your tax preparer can keep you abreast of any shifts in the regulations.

Help With Bitcoin Taxes

Bitcoin is still so recent that the tax guidelines are seldom clear. There are services that can assist Bitcoin users to calculate the total tax that could be due or payable. Unfortunately, you won't find them in every country. While little has been forthcoming, similar services are almost guaranteed to become available worldwide over time.

Bitcoin Worldwide Regulations

In the same way that taxation on Bitcoin differs from one country to another, so do the regulations. There are even some countries where the regulations will vary from one state to another. As far as regulations are concerned, there are no set rules and the chances are that some countries will not regulate Bitcoin at all.

Currently there are few countries where Bitcoin regulations are enforceable. Many countries have issued warnings with regards to Bitcoin. It is usually positioned as educating people about its risks and attempting to clarify that no central authority exists to oversee bitcoin transactions.

Is the world truly ready for this disruptive new technology? Only time will tell. However, giving total financial control to a distributed system instead of relying on centralized institutions and services is a massive shift within the financial world. It is therefore no surprise that most financial services and governments are very wary of what may come. Of course, the emergence on the scene of a new competitor who could cut into their profits may also bear weight.

Even though numerous countries have accepted bitcoin on some level, whether taxed or not, this form of currency could impact, positively or negatively, all existing financial services, in a big way.

BitLicense

It is unlikely that applying existing financial regulations to Bitcoin will work; chances are, this would not be to anyone's advantage. One example of this sort of application is the New York BitLicense. Although

Bitcoin experts were on hand during its development, the rules for Bitcoin – which many users in the Bitcoin community have classed as unreasonably harsh – were drafted by a central authority,

The main concerns regarding the BitLicense regulation are the vast guidelines that require users to make their information public. A vast number of Bitcoin leaders regard this as intrusive and feel strongly that customers' information should be kept private. As a result, many companies have withdrawn their services from New York State.

In order to apply for a BitLicense, one must cough up a non-refundable fee of $5,000, as well as legal fees that could exceed $20,000. When a BitLicense is applied for it has no guarantee of acceptance. In addition, some Bitcoin companies would be expected to provide every detail with regards to their business and their customers.

BitLicense regulations also contain some form of anti-money-laundering guidelines in conjunction with federal rules. If this were not enough, some Bitcoin companies are scrutinized more harshly than traditional institutions, institutions that have amassed a history of corruption, fraud and bad management of customers' funds.

While regulating bitcoin will make great headway toward legitimizing it as a form of legal tender, personally I think BitLicense is a negative example, portraying how *not* to do things. Not only will these regulations stunt the growth of Bitcoin in New York, the excessive cost to obtain a license will not even be an option for most other countries.

In the grand scheme of things, $25,000 may seem reasonable to legalize a business in New York, however, many companies are looking long-term. As more companies comply this will be seen as attractive to other states; this could mean a cost in excess of $1,000,000 to establish a license for all 50 states.

When they refused to comply with BitLicense regulations and closed their services in New York State, many bitcoin firms have sent out an unequivocal proclamation. They are communicating that the regulation of Bitcoin is positive, but attempting to simply copy a traditional style of financial regulations will not work. Certainly, slapping regulations on bitcoin with the addition of an excessively high application fee will definitely not work.

Regulations In Other Places

Other countries are not making great headway toward regulating cryptocurrencies. Finland and the Netherlands have announced that capital gains tax will be assessed to bitcoin, but no details have yet been provided. The two countries are sticking to these regulations until the EU decides whether or not it will regulate bitcoin.

Some Asian nations are trying to completely stop bitcoin from being used by third party processors. There are no official laws banning bitcoin in Asia, apart from Vietnam. However, central banks in the region are being discouraged from getting involved.

In the years to come, Bitcoin regulation will mature into a shape that I believe will be adopted en masse for all forms of digital currency. The best place to start, in my opinion, would be to open up discussions between Bitcoin experts and regulators.

License To Transmit Money

The issue that is keeping bitcoin users on their toes at this writing concerns whether the local government thinks of them as transmitters of money. A money transmitter is a business that supplies payment instruments, in other words, a money transfer service.

We know bitcoin can be traded, spent and bought. This makes it a valuable way to transmit money all over the world. Yet, if individual bitcoin users are viewed as money transmitters, regulations may require them to hold a transmitter license in the future, adding another layer of complexity to the system.

Bitcoin miners, however, are treated differently. Users who create additional bitcoin and sell them to other users for hard currency – or an equivalent – are classified as money transmitters, but they are not regulated at all.

Bitcoin exchange operators essential for translating bitcoin into local currency, can be defined as a business and subjected to all the applicable taxes. The one notable exception is the Isle of Man, which requires exchanges to comply with all relevant guidelines set by the island's flexible spending account rules. Under current guidelines, this core activity of the Bitcoin system requires no license.

Build Your Own

Several governments are looking to build their own cryptocurrencies, but so far, no national-based form of cryptocurrency has been successfully established.

- Estonia is working to roll out its own currency, the "estcoin."
- Kazakhstan is in the process of closed testing on its proposed digital currency. The country threatened to ban other forms of virtual currency, but I believe that idea has been dropped. Plenty of exchanges exist around the area that will swap your Kazakh tenge for bitcoin. In addition, you can now use bitcoin to pay for any traffic violations you acquire when you travel through the country.
- Japan is working on the J-coin, its own brand of cryptocurrency.

Bitcoin Banned And Banished!

Here are the most notable countries that have declared against Bitcoin and usually against other cryptocurrencies as well:

- **Algeria** – As of this writing, the country is considering legislation that would proclaim a total ban on all forms of digital currency; not only will trading be illegal, but so will ownership.
- **Bangladesh** – You can be thrown in jail for owning any decentralized digital currency.
- **Bolivia** – The central Bolivian bank has banned any coins and currencies that have not been issued or regulated by the Bolivian government. In 2014, a policy was issued, warning that the use of any currency apart from that issued and under the control of the government of Bolivia is illegal. I don't think any form of cryptocurrency will be used in Bolivia any time soon.

- **Columbia** forbids the use of or investment in bitcoin.
- **Ecuador** banned Bitcoin and all other types of decentralized digital money back in 2014. It was at this same time that the National Assembly of Ecuador announced guidelines for their own state-run centralized currency. The digital currency was launched in February of 2018, but was shut down shortly thereafter. Still, the Bitcoin ban remains in force, as of this writing.
- **Iceland** holds some different ideas about Bitcoin. Completing transactions with Bitcoin is permitted, yet selling and or buying foreign exchange is strictly prohibited, because it is considered a form of exporting money out of the country.
- **Kyrgyzstan's**, National Bank made its feelings quite clear regarding Bitcoin or any other type of digital currency. Ownership or use is illegal. The only money that constitutes legal tender throughout the country is the Kyrgyz som.
- **Nepal** banned Bitcoin from use in 2017.

Many other countries worldwide are as yet undecided but they're watching Bitcoin to gauge the kind of difference it could have on their economy. Only time will tell on which side of the fence these countries will land.

Chapter 11: Why Trust Bitcoin?

Trust is always the greatest obstacle to embracing new technology. Bitcoin calls for trust to work both directions. Even though, as a user, you have full control of your own bitcoin, the system itself calls for a level of trust. For example, I have learned one valuable lesson in life: nothing is certain. How do we know the entire Bitcoin network will not just up and disappear overnight?

One major assurance comes in its track record. Thus far, the Bitcoin platform has not even wobbled in performance. For almost two decades, it has steadily served participants. Even with wide value fluctuations, Bitcoin appears firmly established. It gives every indication of enduring for the foreseeable future.

The Bitcoin network contains so many individual users and it has established so many solid Bitcoin nodes at this point that the network would be nearly impossible to destroy. At last count, there are just shy of five million bitcoin users and around seven thousand bitcoin nodes. Those are not huge figures, in comparison to credit card users or other cryptocurrencies, but neither are they unsubstantial. A significant proportion of the world's population has chosen to trust Bitcoin; that should weigh heavily in its favor.

Most people have the greatest difficulty trusting Bitcoin's model of decentralization. While some find it disconcerting that there's no one person to hold responsible should problems arise, decentralization actually works in our favor. It minimizes the chances that a dictator could hijack the system and skew it to advantage only a portion of the users.

Bitcoin has no central hinge-point that is subject to failure. Since the authority for transactions is shared across the network, no individual is able to take down Bitcoin entirely. Each individual user makes up a valuable presence in the system. An incredibly complicated strategy involving widespread collaboration would be required in order to shut down everything all at once.

Yet, there is one facet of Bitcoin that rightly makes people think twice before committing their funds to Bitcoin. Because no central authority oversees the Bitcoin network, if something *does* go wrong, there is nobody to whom you can appeal for help. The solid fact remains that bitcoin transactions are irreversible. Once you've spent your bitcoin, there's no way to get them back. Of course, if you're dealing with a known party (such as a business), you can always appeal to that party to initiate a refund transaction. In that respect Bitcoin is no different from other financial transactions you make every day, transactions that are not normally reversible.

Bitcoin As A Change Agent

As humans, we are wired to prefer the status quo and to reject change. After all, change can be dangerous. Yet, without change, we'd still be back in the Stone Age struggling to make fire.

When the internet first came into our lives, very few people could envision it becoming the household staple that it is today. Back then, the internet was just for geeks. Yet, look at how far it has come! Today, everybody and his dog (or cat) is on the internet!

Our lives are bound up in the internet. Without our technology, we can actually feel naked, exposed disoriented like we're flying blind through life. In just a few short years, the internet has totally reshaped our lives to the point that we wouldn't know what to do without instant digital connection to everything and everyone.

We can liken today's Bitcoin to the early internet. Like Bitcoin, the internet was once viewed as a new and disruptive technology. It was considered too advanced for its time. Detractors doubted that the internet would find widespread applicability, just as today few people can see Bitcoin becoming an enduring part of society's mainstream.

One reason its potential is so underrated is that Bitcoin is solving technological problems that most people have never experienced. This is not because of a lack of evidence, it is simply that few of us grasp the extent to which cryptocurrencies can make our lives better. Like the internet, as we perceive its usefulness, Bitcoin will grow into an essential presence in our everyday lives.

The distributed ledger structure of the blockchain has potential that extends far beyond its function as the guardian of Bitcoin transactions. We're already exploring its potential to keep sensitive data from getting lost. Currently, most important information is being stored in a central repository. The problem is, what if something happens to that repository? This is where the blockchain and other distributed ledger systems can prove invaluable.

Only you can decide whether you should put your trust in Bitcoin. Bitcoin has always had the sole intention of ensuring that people have full control of their money. If you choose to embrace this freedom, it comes with responsibility. The rest of this book is designed to help you gain the skills you need to responsibly manage your funds, under the freedom afforded by Bitcoin.

Bitcoin as Currency

Regular currencies can be backed by governments or can be backed by commodities such as silver or gold. Cryptocurrencies are backed by cryptographic mathematical formulas and are supported by the communities that participate in their mode of exchange. In this way, Bitcoin shares characteristics of a form of currency:

- Durability and permanence.
- Portability, the ability to use it in multiple places.
- Scarcity. It's finite.
- Divisibility; it can be subdivided into parts. Each bitcoin is divisible up to 100 million times.
- Exchangeability. Any currency can be exchanged for services, products, or other forms of currency.

The key to a currency's success is its growing adoption and acceptability. The success of Bitcoin depends on the growing number of individuals who invest in it. In addition, its increasing acceptance by reputable businesses as a form of payment, lends credence to its trustworthiness.

Any currency's usefulness depends on how easily it can be accessed. The key exchange point for local currencies is the bank and increasingly, the ATM. Interestingly, Bitcoin ATMs are now cropping up around the world.

Here's a recent snapshot showing the quantity of ATMs accessible in various countries:

- USA – 1,595
- Canada – 420
- Austria – 136
- UK – 116
- Czech Republic - 40
- Spain – 40
- Russian Federation – 39
- Australia – 24
- Switzerland – 22
- Finland – 21

In April 2017, the headlines read, "Bitcoin accepted in 260,000 stores this summer in Japan!" This serves to illustrate Bitcoin's rapidly growing acceptability and adoption by the retail sector. .

Bitcoin's worth is based on the same rationales and principles as all other currencies and commodities. Its success or failure depends on the confidence and trust of those using it. If people and eventually financial institutions and banks believe a currency has value, it has value.

The next big price hike could provide massive profits for those who invested early in digital currencies. When this happens the financial institutions, banks and government will begin to look upon digital currencies as a valid commodity, when this happens these institutions will begin to invest thus adding more value.

April and May 2017 saw a huge increase to bitcoin value, this could have been because Japan adopting Bitcoin as a way to pay and this was adopted by vast numbers of retailers. If this price increase is indicative of future acceptance, we really could be at the beginning of something bigger than our wildest expectations.

History has shown that currencies do collapse and digital currencies like other currencies could follow in the same vein. However, it is worth remembering that most failing currencies have collapsed by human intervention or the inability and failure to manage the currency responsibly.

The financial collapse of 2008 and 2009 occurred because of the excessive greed of bankers, who offered what looked like great deals on what were in reality known as "toxic stock." Even though all the governments with their regulations and codes of conduct were complicit or oblivious. These businesses took money from people even though they were aware that they would be the only ones to make a profit at the people's expense. When we ask ourselves how or why this happened it was us, the public trusting them. Do we still have this faith in them? This is up to our own choice, however, for those who lost their savings and retirement funds to the organizations may have something more to say on the matter.

The financial institutions and banks will lay the blame on anything or anybody rather than except it was their fault. The currencies didn't collapse due to a free market, but because of their greed and involvement in the free market for their own exclusive benefit, currencies were their toys and any profit was theirs and theirs alone.

So regular currency as in the hard cash that you invest can become worthless and disappear because of human intervention and greed. Bitcoin however is run by cryptography and may in the long run become more stable than our accepted types of currency.

Bitcoin and other currencies are generally a completely different type of currency and they have fewer weaknesses or disadvantages than regular currencies. Digital currencies function without there being any chance of human intervention that flat currencies are exposed to. No single agencies controls Bitcoin therefore it only reacts to the impulses of digital currency markets and the users.

It is the shared responsibility amongst those trading in digital currencies that keep the currency buoyant and it has survived and grown immensely since 2009. Currently, since it is very early in the life of digital currencies there is no knowing where it will lead to, it is all speculation and superstition, but at this moment in time it is generating unheard profits for some.

Any investment is a gamble, but a calculated gamble where you invest only what you can live without, is your choice. The digital currency is flourishing at this moment in time since it has for the past few years, but as quickly as things come up they can also go down and provided you keep this in mind you can't go wrong. There is a possibility that a lesser known coin will pass Bitcoin in price and future profits, although currently this seems highly unlikely. If this did happen and people began moving from Bitcoin to another currency the reaction could be harsh and may cause Bitcoin to lose part or even all of its value.

Ponzi Schemes

Those familiar with Ponzi schemes know them as a deceitful investment strategy where a manipulator pays investors returns out of new funds provided by new investors, from profits that have been earned from legitimate investment sources. Ponzi schemes will only exist if there are new investors to pump new funds into the scheme.

Probably the largest Ponzi scheme so far uncovered was run by Bernard Madoff. Madoff was treated as an icon of American financial success by Wall Street and with this accolade the value of his name alone had big investors begging him to take their money. He earned millions until everything came crashing down around his ears. He is now in prison, sentenced to 100 years and his reputation is in tatters.

The value of all currencies is determined by its power to act as a medium of exchange. If people choose to use it, it has value. Digital currencies however have one major difference from all commodities and other currencies and this is the Blockchain since it keeps an unchangeable ledger which is available for everybody to see. It records every transaction ever made and it is because of this that Bitcoin can function seamlessly with no intervention human or otherwise. Do you think your bank would divulge this amount of transparency if asked?

When you look at greed in relation to digital currency, it is just in the speculative nature of this new form of currency or those wanting to set up a Ponzi style scheme outside the Blockchain. All Ponzi schemes will collapse eventually in their entirety and some people will be left penniless while the scheme's originators walk away with pockets full of other trusting, gullible people's money.

It goes without saying if a scheme is laying out more than is made it will run out of money. This is obvious and means that all Ponzi schemes need an ever-growing collection of new investors so that payments to the older members can be maintained, therefore, when the new investors dry up, the originators eventually reach the point where they wind down the scheme and make off with the proceeds. The only thing that cannot be predicted is when the scheme will collapse.

Bitcoin Is No Ponzi Scheme

There are several reasons why Bitcoin cannot be defined as a Ponzi scheme:

- Bitcoin will still have value even when people stop buying them.
- Bitcoin doesn't pay any dividends to the individuals who own coins.
- Bitcoin does not entice new investors to join.
- Bitcoin can't be defined as a company; it has no CEO, no corporate headquarters.
- Unlike a Ponzi scheme, there is no central command of Bitcoin.
- Bitcoin is completely transparent.

The Advantages Of Bitcoin As A Currency

Unlike a commodity such as gold, bitcoin is:

- Easy to transfer
- Easy to verify
- Easy to keep secure
- Easy to make into smaller units

Unlike currencies, bitcoin is:

- Predictable and finite

- Not controlled by a central authority such as financial institutions, banks and governments
- Not based on debt

Unlike electronic currency systems, bitcoin:

- Is anonymous
- As an asset, cannot be frozen
- Offers fast transfers – in seconds instead of days
- Requires no transfer or intermediary fees

Governments cannot demand more bitcoin to be produced. Blocks are only created by mining. This in turn helps support the network because miners are rewarded with bitcoin and transaction fees that others have paid.

Markets will never become flooded by bitcoin. Although bitcoin cannot be destroyed they can be lost, but outside the Blockchain no new rules can be applied to the Bitcoin, giving the advantage to any one party over another. No manipulation can take place as Bitcoin is totally decentralized. Bitcoin is also off the financial grid which means that governments cannot create fees, taxes, levies and so on.

Easy Mobile Payments With Bitcoin

By having Bitcoin on your mobile, you have the freedom to pay by simply scanning and paying. Unlike other payment methods you are not required to sign up to a program, you don't need a password or to swipe a card. By displaying the QR code in your personal Bitcoin wallet application just need to scan your cell phone in the paying and receiving device. No more worrying when you have forgotten your purse, as rarely do people today go anywhere without their mobile phone.

Secure Control Of Your Money

Military grade cryptography is deployed across all Bitcoin transactions. Nobody can charge you a fee or make payments on your behalf provided you use the necessary security to protect your wallet. Done properly, you will have an extremely high level of security.

Anytime, Anywhere

Bitcoin never closes. It is open 24 hours a day, 365 days a year. It never shuts for maintenance and cannot be affected by industrial action or lack of staff. Bitcoin just keeps on going.

Your Bitcoin wallet gives you the opportunity to send funds anywhere worldwide. Bank transfers can take days and incur fees, but Bitcoin payments are practically instant with no fees or hidden charges. You can send and receive an unlimited amount of transactions.

Incentives, Not Fees

Receiving bitcoin incorporates no fees. When you spend bitcoin though, you may choose to offer miners an incentive in order to speed up its processing. The situation is the same as the postage fees you may pay to get your online purchases sent faster. When you buy something online, often the merchant will offer free shipping. However, if you want to receive your purchase sooner than the standard two weeks, you can opt to pay more for faster processing.

Your Identity Protected

Bitcoin has no card number that criminals can use to pretend they are you. You can send a payment without revealing who you are in almost the same way you can use physical money. I cannot reiterate enough that it's up to you to protect your privacy. Still, bitcoin is as secure as any other currency.

With bitcoin, you have full control of your funds at all times; this is the basic ethos of Bitcoin. It is this aspect that scares many, as banks and governments have been taking care of our security for all our lives and we're used to letting them. It can be a burden to manage our money ourselves and many people do not want this type of responsibility.

I freely admit that not everybody is ready for the self-determination demanded by bitcoin. If you are not prepared to set aside some time and effort in order to manage your money down to the smallest detail, bitcoin is not for you.

However, if you are tired of banks, governments and current financial systems managing your money to their own advantage instead of yours, Bitcoin is well worth the time and effort. I am not saying that you should replace all your local currency with bitcoin, but there's plenty of room for both systems to comfortably coexist. Once you begin to see the benefits if using bitcoin for purchases, you'll taste not only the excitement of a good deal, but more importantly the true financial freedom that Bitcoin provides.

Chapter 12: The Top Ten Uses For Bitcoin

Now, we'll look at ways you can invest in and spend your bitcoin.

The only limit to Bitcoin at this moment in time, regards payment. However, as it grows in popularity and more retailers will accept it, soon it will be common to buy anything, using the coin. Whether you want to educate others about this type of digital currency, use it to make an extra income, or simply want to invest in it, bitcoin gives you the freedom to do almost anything with ti. For this reason, I am dedicating this chapter to what I consider to be the ten best ways you can use bitcoin. Of course, the field is constantly changing and new opportunities are opening up every day, so you'll want to stay alert to other possibilities. Still, these uses are valid and will continue to be applicable for the near future.

Bitcoin As Investment

The majority of people regard bitcoin as a form of future investment. With its supply capped at twenty-one million coins and its relatively low price, there are many ways you can turn a profit just by investing in Bitcoin. While it is admirable if you want to play the bitcoin market for quick profits, keep in mind that losses can appear as quickly as profits.

You can also apply bitcoin as investment by including it in your future planning, not just as a way to make a quick gain. Bitcoin is still relatively new; it is fairly undeveloped, so there is plenty to discover. This makes bitcoin a good investment portal, albeit a risky one.

Bitcoin Education

In my opinion, the main purpose of Bitcoin is to educate people about the blockchain and show them its huge potential to help them control the use of their own money. It also serves to change the way people interact with technology and, to some degree, how they view the rest of the world.

Fraud can be found everywhere, as is bad management, restrictions on finances, limits on what constitutes free speech and much more that really should not be allowed in today's world. Satoshi Nakamoto first

125

conceived of the cryptocurrency as one method to promote a disruptive form of technology that would show people that they could decentralize their entire lifestyle so they could live free from fraud and corruption.

Until now, most of the focus of Bitcoin education has been on the technological and financial aspects. While there is still much room for improvement, Bitcoin has vast potential to improve lives. It goes a lot further than technology and finance. The potential is outstanding. Once you fully comprehend how Bitcoin and blockchains function, you will be able to imagine the value it can add to your day-to-day life.

The possibilities are endless. Take a few minutes to think about how elections could be managed with no actual human oversight. Just imagine the ability to sign and store documents, amending and negotiating contracts, and the way in which peer to peer transactions can take place. All these can be provided, safely and securely, using blockchain technology.

Everyday Spending

People are primarily attracted to Bitcoin because it provides an online method for making payments. Businesses are beginning to accept bitcoin payments, thanks to the low cost involved, the low risk of chargebacks or fraud and the possibility for instant transactions. Thanks to this, bitcoin is making its mark as a feasible form of payment, both online and in many stores worldwide. The Bitcoin system is mainly used today to send funds to any place in the world. However, its growth in business acceptance only adds to its viability.

An interesting option for spending Bitcoin manifests itself as businesses that provide food delivery right to your door. The coffee chain, Starbucks, now accepts bitcoin payments, as does Domino's Pizza (PizzaForCoins.com). Online giants like Microsoft and Expedia, lead a host of online stores. Dish Network, CheapAir and Roadway Moving accept bitcoin payments for their services. As of this writing, more than a thousand storefronts around the world will accept payment in bitcoin; this includes restaurants, pubs, museums, and more. If you conduct a quick search of the internet you will see that there are many ways to spend your bitcoin.

Bitcoin And Luxury Expenses

Unsurprisingly, bitcoin has attracted people from a wide range of backgrounds. From millennials to citizens of underdeveloped economic areas, people can now become a part of a brand-new financial creation. You can secure hotel and flight bookings using bitcoin. You can also use it to pay bills and even pay off traffic tickets in a few places. Plenty of services are available to facilitate this process.

The companies that do accept bitcoin have reported that customers who pay with bitcoin happily spend a little more on their hotels and flights. This may be because they feel more comfortable spending larger amounts; alternatively, it could be that the exchange rate at the time was dreadful. We don't yet know why, but it does prove that accepting Bitcoin is beneficial to both buyer and seller. This holds true, regardless of the product or service being offered.

Nonprofits Welcome Bitcoin

An especially important thing in life is our ability to help others, particularly the most needy. A variety of charities, including Greenpeace and the Red Cross, accept donations made in bitcoin. Some charities are also prepared to assist the donor with processing their bitcoin donations as a tax deduction.

Thanks to bitcoin, you can now send your donations directly to people in need, instead of relying on a third party to do this for you. For example, following the 2015 Nepal earthquake, several people were able to give bitcoin directly to the Nepal Relief Fund, instead of filtering their donations through charitable organizations in their home country. The bitcoin donations were quickly available at the disaster site, allowing crisis workers to address critical needs immediately without having to wait for funds to roll in via more traditional methods.

Online Gambling

There are still a few places where sports betting and online gambling are not legal, you will want to pay attention to applicable regulations and rules. If, however, online gambling is legal in your area, bitcoin is a faster and simpler way to pay, instead of using bank cards and or bank transfers.

With bitcoin, you won't need to provide personal information and or other documentation to verify your identity. You'll deposit your funds and you are ready to play! Because bitcoin transfers are non-refundable and rapid, this makes it the ideal payment method for online casinos. While I appreciate that you are a responsible adult, my conscience still requires me to remind you to gamble responsibly. Enough said!

Precious Metal Investment

You can use bitcoin for buying gold, silver and other precious metals. A number of platforms allow you to trade bitcoin against precious metals. Currently the most popular online platform is Vaultoro and this platform has a focus which is mainly on Bitcoin and gold. Uphold, Midas Rezero and BitGold are three other solid platforms where Bitcoin can be used to trade for precious metals. Before you invest any of your Bitcoin be sure to research the companies you are intending to use and their reputation.

Gifting Bitcoin

Bitcoin makes an ideal gift for friends and family and there are many sites where bitcoin can be exchanged for gift cards, such as eGifter and Gyft. Bitcoin can be used through a number of most merchants, even though most of them do not accept direct Bitcoin payments. However, thanks to gift cards, bitcoin can be gifted directly or used as a method of payment for other cards.

Bill Payments

Whether you can pay your bills using Bitcoin will depend on where you live. There are several platforms currently being developed which will allow people to pay any of their bills using Bitcoin for just a small commission.

In the near future, it will be possible to pay your mortgage, phone and utility bills using Bitcoin. It has been possible to top up your mobile phone using Bitcoin for quite a long time, although, this function is not available in all areas of the world just yet.

Expanding the Bitcoin Community

Assuming you have a real passion for Bitcoin but are disheartened by the lack of usability currently. What is stopping you from going out and educating consumers and merchants about the many benefits they could benefit from by using and or accepting Bitcoin? Developing the Bitcoin ecosystem will take vast amounts of time and effort and since no centralized authority manages things, it's up to the Bitcoin community users to spread the word and push for the adoption of Bitcoin.

All of the Bitcoin uses outlined here represent just a small proportion of the possibilities. By thinking up your own ways of using the virtual currency Bitcoin, it provides a lot of value to the Bitcoin community. It is also important to share how you can use Bitcoin every time you are able to with the community.

Chapter 13: Altcoins: All The Other Cryptocurrencies

Because Bitcoin was the first, every other form of cryptocurrency has been dubbed an altcoin, or an alternative form of digital coinage. Yes, it's time to talk about the other guys. You're going to learn in what follows how to trade across multiple cryptocurrencies. You will also gain considerable insight into the altcoin community and be able to crowdfund and gamble using various cryptocurrencies, if you are so inclined.

How To Evaluate Them All

Deciding which altcoin is "best" is like deciding on what kind of dessert to choose. How do you decide whether to cap off your meal with a luscious piece of melt-in-your-mouth cheesecake or a slice of scrumptious pie? Add in brownies a la mode, peach crisp, rich sorbet, Mediterranean baklava, flan, etc. And you've a dilemma of major proportions on your hands. It's an altcoin-sized challenge.

With any financial decision, there are any number of variables to consider. If you measure success by sheer number of transactions processed per second, you would come up with a short-list that looks something like this (I've included Visa as a comparison to the "real" world of commerce):

1. Visa   24,000
2. Ripple   1,500
3. PayPal   193
4. Bitcoin Cash   60
5. Litecoin   56
6. Dash   48
7. Ethereum   20
8. Bitcoin   7
9.

By this valuation, you'd be ahead to just use your credit card.

Instead of usage numbers, you might prefer to compare a coin's market share. Here's a recent snapshot of digital currency standings, based on descending market capitalization:

1. Bitcoin   107G
2. Ethereum   20G
3. XRP   17G
4. Stellar   4G
5. LTC   3G
6. Cardano   1.9G
7. Monero   1.6G
8. Dash   1.3G

The time elapsed before the next block is released will have a huge impact on how quickly you can transact business. Here's a recent snapshot, showing how long transactions took on average, in minutes:

1. Bitcoin   12.973
2. Litecoin   2.88
3. Dash   2.63
4. ZCash   2.496
5. Monero   1.96
6. Dogecoin   1.039
7. Auroracoin   0.876
8. Ethereum   0.237

By this measure, you'd go with anything *but* Bitcoin.

If you're thinking in terms of how much it will cost you to actually use these digital currencies, Bitcoin is by far and away the most expensive. Monero is less expensive, but still can rack up considerable transaction fees over time. Everybody else charges next to nothing by comparison.

Today, multitudes of developers are hoping to create the next big splash in the cryptocurrency market; they dream of overtaking Bitcoin. In the past few years, thousands of altcoins have appeared on the scene. However the majority disappear almost as quickly as they show up.

You'll want to watch out for "scamcoins." Wherever you find legitimate financial opportunities, you'll also find unscrupulous vendors out to make a fast buck off of players who may not be alert to potential danger. Some scamcoins amount to a "pump then dump" scheme; they're introduced to turn a fast profit and then shut down. Other legitimate altcoins have been launched but were pulled quickly because of design flaws that showed up early in implementation. Any emerging form of digital coinage may have small chance of catching up with Bitcoin's standing in the market, but there is no shortage of contenders. Some of them have even gained considerable ground on the frontrunner.

With thousands of altcoins jostling for position in the market and many more under development at any given time, it's an impossible task to describe – let alone track – them all. Instead, this chapter will review eight legitimate digital currencies that have emerged, just to showcase the diversity of products available. This is not an endorsement; you'll have to do your own research to decide what altcoin best suits your needs at the moment.

Litecoin (LTC) – Improving On Bitcoin

When it first emerged in 2011, two years after Bitcoin appeared, the hype was all about Litecoin being "the silver to Bitcoin's gold." While it has much to commend it as we shall see, the original altcoin is currently only one amid a plethora of possibilities.

Litecoin began its existence as a hived-off "fork" of Bitcoin. A major change in the way an algorithm works will call for the start of an entirely new entity. In this case, the "fork" became known as Litecoin because at first glance it appears to be nothing more than a lightweight version of Bitcoin. However, this altcoin has some major advantages over its parent:

- Its speed blows Bitcoin out of the water. Instead of waiting 10 minutes for transaction confirmation, Litecoin does it in 2.5 minutes. This is a huge boost for retailers. However, as we've seen already, the standard for block release time is now reduced to a few seconds, so this is only an advantage when we're comparing it to Bitcoin.

- Litecoin pioneered the use of the Scrypt hashing algorithm. This is also an advantage over Bitcoin that doesn't hold in comparison with other alternatives.
- Litecoin was the first cryptocoin to adopt SegWit, a security feature that "segregates" the "witnesses" and removes them from the blockchain. This allows for faster block processing and greater overall security. Now that Bitcoin and other altcoins are adopting SegWit in its various iterations, this is also less of an advantage.
- It's popular in China. The Chinese comprise one of the world's largest market blocks, so its massive acceptance among this people offers a huge advantage to future growth.
- It's less volatile than Bitcoin. Litecoin is less apt to be affected by market corrections.
- It has a greater number of potential coins. Litecoin has a capacity of 84 million coins, compared to Bitcoin's 21 million.

Litecoin has remained relevant. It now boasts a loyal, committed community that continues to grow rapidly.

The majority Litecoin's success, apart from its processing speed, comes from its consistent presence at every cryptocurrency exchange. Litecoin these days can be traded on most cryptocurrency exchanges available today. In addition, several payment processors now include Litecoin and provide their community with ways to spend Litecoin along with Bitcoin.

Dogecoin (DOGE) – Unlimited Supply

In 2013, when Dogecoin launched, it appeared to be a "meme" coin, because its image was portrayed in cartoon style. This altcoin has no cap on its currency. As long as miners are willing to work at it, new dogecoin will be added. Because it lacks a cap on supply, Dogecoin was never expected to rise to the status of a major cryptocurrency.

However, it shines by sheer speed and number of transactions completed. Its ease of use has led to this altcoin being offered as awards in online competitions, used to purchase currency in online games and to tip service providers. Dogecoin is proud of its roots as a community cryptocurrency; the efforts of the combined community have raised funds for a number of beneficial causes.

Dash (DASH) - Anonymity

As you've been reading this book, you've probably noticed that anonymity is big in this field. Bitcoin is unable to offer complete anonymity, but it does offer pseudonymity. Users are able to hide their identity with their wallet address. Yet this weakness, the lack of true anonymity, has fueled many developers to invent alternative solutions to the problem.

While the current leader of anonymity at the moment is Monero, plenty of anonymous altcoins also exist. These include Zcash, PIVX, Komodo, Zcoin, NAV Coin, ZenCash and Verge, to name a few. Another solution to offer greater anonymity than Bitcoin is Dash.

When it burst upon the scene in 2014 under the name Darkcoin, Dash was a leader in providing anonymity. The main developer of Dash, Evan Duffield, offered several solutions to give users complete anonymity and to provide for anonymous transactions. Dash is still a popular anonymous altcoin.

Ripple (XRP) – Banking On...Banks

Most cryptocurrencies are built upon decentralization. However Ripple – created and maintained by Ripple Labs, Inc. – has been partnering with banking institutions since its emergence in 2012. Banks love Ripple because transactions are fast, it can handle all the traffic you want to hand it (at peak times processing as many transactions per second as Visa) and the platform has performed flawlessly from day one, balancing its open ledgers with nary a hiccup.

Peercoin (PPC) – Proof Of Stake Transactions

Bitcoin and Litecoin share one characteristic in common: the only way new coins can be generated is through mining. Peercoin, an early Bitcoin clone, offered a new way to release coins known as "proof-of-stake transactions." The proof-of-stake determination occurs when a user hodls – or holds onto - coins in their wallets for a period of time without spending anything.

With Peercoin, as the coins reach a certain age, they will have amassed a small amount of interest, which is returned to the owner of the original peercoins. The whole process is the same as with a bank savings account, except that it remains decentralized, with users remaining in full control of their funds at all times.

When you go through the process of making more peercoins, using proof-of-stake determination, you are increasing the stability of the platform while decreasing the number of miners required to keep everything running. There will always be users wanting to stake their peercoins. In addition, the developers of Peercoin have been able to steadily apply 1% inflation each year with no coin cap in place.

StartCOIN (START) – For Crowdfunding

StartCOIN is reward-based, established on the crowdfunding model. This coin allows users to make a pledge to share and hold StartCOIN on the website. Coins, are rewarded for various activities.

Crowdfunding has gained huge popularity. StartCOIN has taken full advantage of this trend, encouraging communities to fund various concepts, ideas and projects. Users who give or receive funding through the website also receive rewards in the form of additional StartCOINs. Still, this altcoin is a newcomer, so little history is available and its future trajectory is unknown.

NXT (NXT) – Coin Without Mining

NXT uses proof-of-stake protocol to arrive at transaction consensus; almost everyone else relies on mining. As a rare cryptocurrencies that operates entirely without mining, all of the coins were distributed when NXT was launched. With a steady stream of coins readily available, this introduced a new type of ecosystem into the cryptocurrency world.

The altcoin is also unique in that a user can create their own cryptocurrencies within the NXT environment. Any newly titled coins have the full backing of NXT and can be disbursed in multiple ways.

NXT has also introduced features that provide an arbitrary messaging service, the governance of smart contracts and a decentralized peer-to-peer exchange known as MultiGateWay.

CasinoCoin (CSC)

CasinoCoin, launched in 2013, is receiving kudos for operating faithfully within its charter. As the moniker suggests, the coin is closely related to the casino business. It is swiftly growing in acceptance across the online gambling industry.

The coin operates under a modified from of the Ripple code based on a Scrypt algorithm. It is widely trusted by banks worldwide, thanks to its excellent translation pipeline connected to traditional financial institutions. CasinoCoin is also in the process of developing features to combat money laundering and to minimize gambling abuse.

Chapter 14: Bitcoin Millionaires

Being a millionaire is not as unique as it used to be. In 2015, more than 8% of the population of America enjoyed a $1 million net worth. Hitting the million dollar mark remains the number one goal for some Americans; for many, being a millionaire symbolizes total financial freedom.

It is easy to assume that people with millions in the bank got there by earning massive salaries or inheriting money from their families. While this is true in some cases, there are plenty of people who gained their fortune by living frugally, making wise investments and by creating their own opportunities to make money.

In 2012, while sitting in college, what I read led me to believe the world would switch to Bitcoin immediately. I was just one of the lucky few to be exposed to alternative currencies early on. I made a stab at purchasing bitcoin, failed and gave up. But, when CoinBase appeared on the scene, that's when I began buying Bitcoin in earnest.

The key to making vast sums of money with cryptocurrencies resides in altcoins.

Altcoins – The Path To Big Earnings

Chances are everyone has heard of Bitcoin and the value that it appears to be continually gaining. In the last year it has trebled in value and its value has been increasing since its launch in 2008.

Personally, I wanted to buy bitcoin in 2013 when it fell to an all-time low of around $60.00. You may have read many online stories about people who purchased bitcoin years ago when it was valued at $10.00 and cashed out when it rose to $50.00. It is true that you can still purchase bitcoin, sit on it for a next few years and cash it in to make a profit.

Long-term Growth

I agree with a large group of analysts who believe that bitcoin could increase in value over the next few years to $30,000.00. A few predict a high of up to $100,000 in ten years' time; although there have been dips in the value of Bitcoin over the years, they really are of the persuasion that Bitcoin's upward trend has only just begun.

If you do invest in Bitcoin, you may double or triple your money but with Bitcoin galloping toward $6,000 per coin, you may feel like that boat has already sailed without you. My belief is that there are plenty of other options available, particularly if you are open to the use of altcoins.

Picking the right altcoin can yield great returns. If you purchase bitcoin for $4,000 and wait a year for the value to increase to $8,000 you will make 200% profit. However, many altcoins can be purchased for a fraction of that price and may well yield up to 100 times the purchase value in only a few months.

Don't get me wrong. Nobody would claim it is easy to realize these enormous returns. It will take work on your part, a leap of faith and huge amounts of research before choosing the right altcoin. Bitcoin, is a little simpler. There is a track record to rely on; the risk, while still considerable, is less unknown. However, many altcoins can be purchased for just a few cents and it is these cheaper coins that have the best chance of chalking up huge gains. I can verify this, as I have enjoyed some sizeable returns on my altcoin investments.

My Story

You may doubt my claims, but these gains exist and occur a lot more frequently than you might imagine. Let me explain what I did.

At the moment, I hold two coins: Bitcoin and Ethereum. Most of my gains have come from Ethereum, because I was able to buy for $10.00 or less. My rationale was as follows:

- Bitcoin needs to solve its scaling issues; and until it does, other currencies can gain ground, possibly taking the lead over time. The longer it takes for these issues to be resolved, the more the other currencies will grow.
- After completing my research, I decided to invest in Ethereum, as I felt that it best suited my needs. From what I read, I realized it

was important to seek out investments that had utility, not just value.

I used my knowledge to my advantage when investing and it paid off. While there are no certainties with investing, it's right to believe you are capable of achieving at least some success in the process

I use the iOS app and Coin Cap to keep track of my crypto holdings. I like that they can be locked using your fingerprint; this gives you a unique form of security that is very difficult to overcome.

Although I shy away from appearing big-headed, I admit I've joined the list of crypto millionaires. However, I am just a small fish in this very big pond. Most of the other investors own much more than I; some even boast of billions! But if I can do this and be successful, so can you. Although my portfolio is small, I am just charting my first step to bigger and better things.

Chapter 15: Bitcoin Etiquette

I cannot express how important it is to know as much as possible about Bitcoin before you dive in. I am going to run through some critical elements you must understand about Bitcoin. This will lay a solid foundation you can build upon. Bitcoin may appear scary at first, because it is so different from anything else we know. However, I hope with this advice to put you more at ease with handling it.

Use A Secure Wallet

As the name suggests, a wallet is what holds the Bitcoin you receive. Multiple wallet types are now available. Most people use a web-based wallet for their everyday bitcoin transactions, opting to store the rest in a more secure form of wallet that can be backed up and more strongly protected.

Understand The Price Will Vary

Bitcoin prices fluctuate by the minute. There will be times when the road gets very bumpy! Recently, Bitcoin has risen steadily but it has also dipped. Just a few years ago, it was hard to believe that Bitcoin was worth a hundred dollars, yet at the point of this writing, its value stands in excess of $5,000.

Irreversible Transactions

Unlike credit cards or PayPal transactions, Bitcoin payments cannot be reversed. Once you have sent off your Bitcoin payment, it is only the recipient who can initiate a return to you. Therefore, it is vital that you trust the person to whom you are sending your funds.

You'll want to double and triple-check the wallet address to which you are sending a payment. If you make a mistake, there is no central authority you can go to for help.

Growing Pains

Bitcoin is growing rapidly, so there will be changes in the future. New updates may see some providers rethinking their pricing and services.

Confirmations may take longer, fees may increase and any number of other adjustments may occur. Even though the future is quite unknown, if you understand how cryptocurrencies work and follow the basic guidelines that apply to all investments, you will be as safe as it is possible to be in a constantly shifting universe.

Understanding Blockchain And Bitcoin Transactions

To understand Bitcoin, you need to know the elements of the technology that make Bitcoin work and this is known as the Blockchain.

In 2008, Satoshi Nakamoto published a white paper on technology of Bitcoin that detailed the system that runs Bitcoin transactions. Bitcoin is a revolutionary idea and the technology behind it really has the capability to change so much of the world for the better beyond Bitcoin.

Its technological system we call the blockchain. This blockchain has many other uses besides Bitcoin, but this is what it is known for right now. The Blockchain decentralized database holds all the transactions that have even been made using Bitcoin and since no governing body, not even a database, controls matters, the ledger sits on a network that is made up of every computer that runs Bitcoin software. Everyone cooperates to create the network. All of this happens in public and anyone can see the traffic as it happens. It is this level of transparency that is unheard of in the economic system particularly a digital one.

When it comes to disruptive forces it is difficult to imagine something that is more powerful than Bitcoin. This has the capacity to change how data is distributed across the internet and ensure it is kept safe by a huge network of computers. This computer network is working to keep the information secure and out of the hands of fraudsters.

How Bitcoin Transactions Work

You may be surprised that bitcoin do not physically exist and when you think about it logically this is too different from our modern money. The money you see when you view your bank balance online doesn't represent a physical box sitting in the bank with your money in it. In the same way, we wonder nothing that can be defined as, "this is a single Bitcoin."

Instead Bitcoin functions as follows:
You initiate a transaction, it is then grouped with other transactions in a "block" which is cryptographically protected. This block is then sent out to the whole network where miners process them.

Blocks

The blocks of transactions contain everything needed to add new transactions as well as to connect the block to all the previous ones. There are four things that are included in every block:

- Reference to the previous block in the chain
- All the transactions that are being added
- Time stamp
- Proof of work data showing how the new block was created

By having all this information in a single block, the blockchain system can regulate itself and doesn't require supervision. No one is needed to manually check transactions; errors are practically impossible. Once processed, the blocks are "hashed" and it is then impossible to alter them. After they're added to the blockchain, the record stays there forever, recorded on every single computer on the network. This process of duplication renders the blockchain almost the most secure database available.

Confirmation

Successful transactions are confirmed and this is how you know that they are correct. It takes miners approximately 10 minutes to create a new block and add it to the Blockchain. This new block verifies, transfers and is recorded in the public record. Once this process is complete it is considered verified. For additional confirmation, however, many people wait for several confirmations, just to ensure their payment isn't reversed for fraudulent activity.

When using Bitcoin at a store, some merchants may not make you wait, but this does mean that they are risking you providing payment.

Fees

In the same way as all transactional systems there are fees for each transfer using Bitcoin. However, the biggest difference is that fees are not a requirement and are determined by the person sending the funds. Like with the confirmations, the fees are received and processed by those who mine the blocks. Once a new Bitcoin block is successfully created, they collect the fees for all the transactions in that specific block.

The fees are voluntary and the person initiating the transaction determines whether they include a fee or not. But by including a fee they ensure that miners have an incentive to process their transaction. The aim of the fees is that miners will make more from the fees than from creating new bitcoin. It is this that provides miners with a reason to carry on mining even though it will prove more difficult over time. You should note at this point that there are wallets that determine the transaction fee for you.

Receipts

When the Bitcoin system was designed there was nothing put in place to provide receipts for purchases, but we wonder a record of transactions in the Blockchain. This applies primarily to direct online payments; however, you will still receive receipts at stores even though the Blockchain doesn't produce it.

Chapter 16: Boost Your Business With Bitcoin

If you own a business there are a host of opportunities available to you. This chapter will explain how you can welcome Bitcoin into your current business model, to your benefit. In addition to saving money, there are a host of loyal Bitcoin users just waiting for opportunity to spend their bitcoin. Why not tap into this massive market? It's actually simpler to get started than you might imagine

Why Choose Bitcoin?

Many of the problems businesses face today can be solved by using digital currency. I offer just a few of the ways you can boost your business by introducing bitcoin into your operations.

Prevent Fraud

If you have accepted credit card payments, you will understand how frustrating chargebacks can be. Even if you are 100% sure the card owner made the purchase, you will be angered when the card provider charges you for processing a fraudulent payment after you have already sent the goods. They may as well have stolen straight from you. This type of fraud is one of the largest issues faced by online merchants.

What if I told you there is a way to prevent this from ever happening to you again? You can avoid it quite easily with Bitcoin. As we have already explained, once a Bitcoin transaction is initiated it is sent to the entire blockchain for confirmation. Once a Bitcoin transaction is confirmed it cannot be cancelled or reversed.

If you really needed to, you could send a refund to a customer, but they have no power to initiate this process themselves. This means that your business will never experience another chargeback situation. You will never again suffer the indignity of chargeback fees. Never again will a customer be allowed to snatch their payment away from you the moment an order is completed.

Eliminate Fees

You have probably visited a business that doesn't accept credit cards; the processing fees are what makes it impossible for especially smaller companies to transact business via credit. Businesses are saddled with transaction fees the customer never sees. These fees can add up quickly. On average, credit card companies charge two to four percent per transaction, with additional fees on top. This may not seem much, but giving away 4% of each sale does cut into your profit.

In this regard, bitcoin is a real game-changer. It can squash those rates down to less than 1%. Bitcoin usage instantly boosts your revenue. Just by choosing to use it over credit cards you can add up to 5% to your bottom line. Many users report the savings in fees is the main reason they have adopted Bitcoin.

Money Hits Your Pocket Faster

Large international transactions can take a long time to process. It is natural to have to wait longer than a week for an international wire transaction to be confirmed and deposited into the bank. Each time you repeat this procedure it can feel like the transfer has bogged down and may never be completed.

Once again, it's Bitcoin to the rescue. Regardless of the payment size or the distance spanned by the transaction, you can see the funds confirmed and in your wallet in just a few minutes.

This is a huge breakthrough for smaller businesses, which are often unable or unwilling to accept international purchases. Unless you are strong enough to absorb the transaction fees and other complications associated with international transactions, these activities will remain out of your reach. Fortunately, this invisible barrier faced by small business owners is entirely eradicated by Bitcoin.

Aids To Bookkeeping

No one wants to dig through receipts or complete mountains of paperwork each time they need to do some accounting. Honestly, no one relishes complicated bookwork that makes it difficult to track down the various transactions from all the different sources.

While it is extremely important for businesses to maintain clear and accurate records of each transaction they make, Bitcoin will serve as a valuable backup. With Bitcoin, all transactions are open and displayed for all to see. This could be a concern for anyone worried about privacy, but remember, your wallet address doesn't specifically identify you. Only you know for certain which transactions are yours.

Accepting Bitcoin

By now you should understand why accepting Bitcoin payments is a great idea. Next, let's talk about the process of getting set up for bitcoin transactions. It is not as hard as you may think. People are working hard to simplify the process; after all, everyone wants to be the frontrunner in Bitcoin merchant technology.

Processing Payments

The primary Bitcoin payment processors available as of this writing are:
- CoinBase
- BitPay
- Coingate
- Blockchain.info
- CoinsBank
- GoUrl

Coingate allows you to convert payment only into dollars or Euros. Blockchain.info is more difficult to implement than the others, but it is solidly reliable. GoUrl is an open source application based in Dominica. In terms of extended history, stability and ease of use, the first two processors stand out from the crowd, so we'll take a look at each of them individually.

CoinBase

CoinBase is probably the most well-known bitcoin payment processor worldwide. It is massive and handles millions of transactions every day.

It is working hard to become the number one service provider for business owners around the world.

CoinBase has made it simple to exchange Bitcoin or any other form of currency, digital or otherwise. CoinBase automatically converts payments daily. At end of a business day any payments you took in are automatically transferred to your bank account, in your local currency. The transfer will take three days to complete, but this is still quicker than receiving payments from most credit card processors.

CoinBase costs nothing until you exceed one million dollars' worth of transactions. Once you have exceeded this amount, it charges a flat fee of 1%. For most businesses, it will take some time to reach the million dollar threshold, but even when you do, you'll still save a money over other forms of processing.

What makes CoinBase stand out above its competitors is the refund platform they have implemented. CoinBase's refund platform allows you to reverse transactions as easily as you can refund credit card payments. This effectively deals with the only real hassle encountered when processing Bitcoin transactions.

BitPay

BitPay stands a close second to CoinBase as the most widely accepted payment processor. As almost the first payment processor to appear, it boasts a sterling reputation.

This platform makes it a simple matter for a customer to pay you using Bitcoin. Customers can scan a QR code, copy and paste a wallet address, or click a link to pay directly using Bitcoin software. Regardless of a customer's experience level, they can easily purchase from you.

From a business owner's point of view, things could not be simpler. Most shopping cart systems in use can easily adapt to the BitPay processor, whether you are operating from a brick and mortar store or an online business. For websites it involves a single line of code that adds BitPay as an option for processing payments. Brick and mortar stores can use an app that accepts payments separately or one that integrates with their existing system.

BitPay has one benefit over CoinBase: Bitcoin payments are transferred into local currency and will be available in the designated bank account on the following day. This is huge, particularly for businesses that deal with multiple suppliers, many of which want to be paid as swiftly as possible. Boosting your cash flow is just one way BitPay can assist your business.

A helpful conversion system is included as part of the free package that businesses are offered to get themselves set up to start accepting Bitcoin. This is far cheaper than the cost of accepting credit cards. Because you won't need to add any infrastructure beyond what you have already set up, you can go from zero to Bitcoin expert in no time and at no additional cost.

If your business starts to outgrow the free plan offered by BitPay, it offers a very reasonable fee structure. The paid plans include VPN access, QuickBooks and other features that become extremely helpful as your business grows. If you are already a sizeable business, I'd still advise starting out with the free plan, just to familiarize yourself with the system. After you are fully initiated into the processing requirements of your business, you'll be able to easily transition to the plan that works best for you.

Online Stores

Online stores became the initial retailers to accept bitcoin payments, but now anyone can join the revolution. With a few lines of code you'll be ready to receive online payments in a jiffy. The most popular e-commerce platforms are already set up to easily include Bitcoin payment gateways.

Brick And Mortar Stores

Brick and mortar stores will find it easy to add bitcoin payments. If you already use a point of sale system, it is quick and easy to add Bitcoin as a method of payment. If you are using an offline system, this may give you a valid excuse to upgrade for the sake of integrating all your sales and simplifying the bookkeeping process. If an upgrade is not in the cards however, you can still include Bitcoin payments through tablet or cell phone apps. There is plenty of online instruction and help for the small business that wants to get set up for digital currency payments.

Chapter 17: Investing With Bitcoin

Most of us aim to have some money put away for later in life, this money does the work giving you returns for very little effort. Some people choose to invest in a retirement account or stocks because they believe this is a good bet in the long run to provide them with a steady stream of income.

The intervention of Bitcoin has given us a new way of investing and analysts think that this may be better than the traditional ways of investing. But is this true? I am going to show you what it means to invest in Bitcoin and help you to start your own portfolio which is almost sure to provide you with great returns providing you understand what it entails.

Long-Term Investment

When it comes to long-term investments, people immediately think of real estate, stocks, or gold. Yet, what if a disruptive force emerges with major advantages over these forms of investment? Yes, Bitcoin is turning out to be a major game changer.

If you use your bitcoin, but buy more than you sell, you are investing in bitcoin. Not long ago, bitcoin could be purchased for just eight cents. That kind of return on your dollar is unrivalled today. Although you may have missed the initial boom, Bitcoin still can provide an amazing ride to the heights.

As you will see, your goal should be to buy bitcoin with a view to being involved in this for years to come. But can this prove an overall beneficial investment? Can you trust that bitcoin will continue to rise in value? What about the volatility we keep hearing about?

Peak Price

It's nigh to impossible to accurately forecast what bitcoin could be worth in the future. Recently, bitcoin jumped to reach briefly the $10,000 mark. Some analysts believe we are just a few years away from $20,000 or $30,000. The owner of Shape Shift truly believes that by 2021, the cryptocurrency market will have grown tenfold. What would that mean for bitcoin? For starters, if this cryptocoin continues on an upward trend, it could easily surpass the $10,000 mark in 2019, with additional gains to follow.

By the end of November 2019, $300 billion in cryptocurrencies were in circulation, with Bitcoin making up about 66% of the total market. From this point, the future is anyone's guess. With continued growth, the price will continue to rise and periodically to correct itself. The stronger the demand, the higher the price; it really is that simple. Even if bitcoin's growth slows, the ongoing demand will continue to drive gains for those who have committed to staying the course.

Understanding Fluctuations

The dips and swings are critical to understand when you're investing in bitcoin. If you panic easily, you will find yourself selling when you should have held on, limiting your gains and losing out on future potential earnings. Bitcoin will continue its volatility, at least for the middle term, so that's something you'll want to keep in the forefront as you are investing.

Adoption and investment typically occur as part of boom and bust cycles. It's common for bitcoin to rise sharply before crashing back down, depending entirely on the ups and down of other markets. Adoption rates rise and fall in the same way as prices. During periods of rapid adoption, the price increases. When adoption rates slow down, the price drops. This can sometime be hard to predict, adding another layer of complexity to day trading. In the end however, adoption will rise steadily, so keep this trend in mind as you mull over your options.

Watch for movement by the big boys; they can stimulate massive upturns in bitcoin prices. When major players invest in bitcoin, it can lead to sudden price leaps. JP Morgan, American Express and Goldman Sachs are all great examples; they have each made large investments in Bitcoin-related businesses. Their massive purchases of bitcoin have driven up the price for a short time. This kind of commitment also wields a longer-lasting impact. As people see these major players getting involved, it increases bitcoin's trustworthiness, leading to greater adoption, which also boosts prices, but in the form of a delayed swell.

Bad Press

In an average day, bitcoin will fluctuate by 2% or more in value. While few people will pay attention to its wavering, these value fluctuations can be amplified by negative press reports.

Bad press can seriously harm adoption rates and put a damper on prices. With every government regulation, each hint of a security breach, the bitcoin value will waver, regardless of the actual meaning contained in an article.

For example, the FBI shut down the Silk Road exchange in October of 2013, for selling weapons and drugs online. With the widely publicized seizure of bitcoin, concerns were raised that the platform may have been established as a safe haven for illegal activities. Understandably, bitcoin prices plummeted as a result. Of course, the concern was only temporary and prices eventually recovered; however the point remains that bad press – whether warranted or purely rumor – has a powerful impact on the market.

Good Press

Good publicity is always welcomed as great for the entire cryptocurrency ecosystem. It's also a trust-builder for anyone thinking about investing in bitcoin. With each technological breakthrough reported, the system gets better and stronger, more resilient and more attractive. Each story covering banks that invest in bitcoin will stimulate more investment firms to view it as a viable option worthy of their consideration. Each local story about a business accepting bitcoin payments will lead others to do the same. For every positive article published, more people become aware of bitcoin. Adoption drives bitcoin forward and makes continued growth possible, so any good news can bump up the price considerably.

Bitcoin vs. Stocks

For many people, stock investments have been their favored method to achieve long-term gains. This remains a tried and true way to invest, despite – or because of – its level of risk. Now that Bitcoin has burst upon the scene, how does it stack up against these traditional investment vehicles?

Will Bitcoin will ever become more powerful than stocks? Some financial experts are suggesting that bitcoin is a better bet than gold, but this falls short of an endorsement of bitcoin over stocks. Yet, there are ways in which Bitcoin has already proved itself a greater investment opportunity.

First, think of it as currency. With stocks, you can hold them in your portfolio as long as you like. To liquidate stocks, you'll need to sell them through a broker. Only then will you have cash you can use to purchase things.

With Bitcoin there's no broker, no middleman at all. The Bitcoin you stash in your everyday wallet gives you the same return as what you are holding back in cold storage.

Short Trading

Short trading works the same, whether you're dealing in stocks, currencies, or in bitcoin. It's not recommended for people with no trading experience, because it requires having a sense for where things are going. Yet, bitcoin is no more risky than any other trading vehicle.

Simply put, short-term trading consists of purchasing bitcoin at a low price and selling it at a higher price, then repeating this process again and again to take advantage of daily, or hourly, price fluctuations. If you can catch the market on the edge of a major change, you can make a quick profit. Then you can reinvest this profit or spend it as you wish.

The volatility of Bitcoin makes it an ideal candidate for a short-term trading strategy. You can trade bitcoin for bitcoin or you can trade across cryptocurrencies. Some altcoins are even growing faster than bitcoin, mostly because they are newer. If you play things right, you can gain a lot of momentum by swapping out cryptocurrencies. With proper, thorough research, people have been able to turn a profit in one currency before catching the wave of another currency's surge.

What Hinders Investors?

Investment analysts are still cautious about recommending bitcoin as an investment. The reasons all boil down to the size of your faith in bitcoin. For those who are pushing for technological innovation, this may not be their primary concern, as they can see the long-term implications of adoption.

The first objection remains that Bitcoin is not backed by anything. Traditional currencies are backed by something that has a tangible value or by the good faith of a governing body. By contrast, bitcoin, is worth however much the populace of the world perceives it to be. Realistically, this means that bitcoin can be highly fickle. Its massive volatility can scare off potential investors.

Bitcoin is not traded on Wall Street, which makes it a bit more complicated. Bitcoin trading is more intensive than regular investing. This can lead to the assumption that Bitcoin is too complex, since it involves much more finagling than other methods. Bitcoin requires a greater level of attention, largely because its market is highly complex. Still, there are fortunes to be made, especially if you do your homework and educate yourself, starting with the tips and resources provided by this book.

Then we have the confusing regulatory status as it appears around the globe. As of this writing, some governments are moving slowly – or not at all – to approve regulations that will welcome bitcoin as a means of investment. While bitcoin investments can be highly lucrative, government regulations can change the scenario overnight, so I recommend keeping one eye on regulatory developments the entire time you are involved in growing your bitcoin.

There's no need to shy away from investing in bitcoin; just investigate the bitcoin environment thoroughly before you dive in. Bear in mind the risks and complications I've already described as you invest in bitcoin, understanding that the adoption rate may be slower than expected. This latter is what wields the greatest influence on its value. Bitcoin truly is a solid investment, although the greatest gains may only appear sometime in the future.

Your Turn

Now that you an idea of what investing in bitcoin means, you can begin to make your own informed decisions. The ways you choose to move forward will depend largely on how much time you are willing to assign to this undertaking. Most people appear to be happy to buy bitcoin and hold onto it for long-term future rewards. You now know there are additional options. May you choose wisely and may you reap wonderful returns on your investments.

Chapter 18: Bitcoin's Future

No one can predict the future and what it may bring. However, the future for bitcoin does appear to be solid. I do predict – in the same vein as most money experts – that Bitcoin will continue to grow, mature and develop, driving increased acceptance of the decentralization model. Some predict the value of Bitcoin will hit $100,000 in the next few years; this adds even more substance to its future prospects.

Energy Futures

Bitcoin will need to overcome several obstacles in order to enjoy continued growth and ongoing viability. One of these obstacles involves the huge amount of energy required needed to keep Bitcoin running. Bitcoin in its current incarnation is extremely inefficient when it comes to energy use. In fact, energy consumption is what could eventually derail the entire operation.

If there are currently 10,000 Bitcoin nodes working to verify transactions, imagine how much energy will be required when the number doubles! Research has shown that just one Bitcoin transaction requires enough energy to power an entire house for 24 hours. Many individual miners and node verifiers have decided not to join the network in these roles, since it would be far too costly for them. Can Bitcoin continue to exist without miners? We simply don't know.

One of the proposed solutions is to alter the protocols so not all nodes will be required to verify a transaction. Yet, this strikes at the core of decentralization and could ultimately endanger the entire system's security, leaving it open to the risk of double spending.

A likely strategy would be to offer nodes incentives to use solar power or other forms of renewable energy. Renewable energy is far cheaper than that derived from fossil fuels. It requires very little, except for the installation of the necessary equipment. One single windmill could power a large mining farm with few costs beyond the initial mounting of the windmill. Where you find enough sunshine, solar panels will produce all sorts of free energy. Incentivizing alternative energy use could provide plenty of power for the existing equipment and reduce its carbon footprint.

Taxation

Another challenge is how various governments will tax or otherwise regulate bitcoin. In the United States, the IRS has declared Bitcoin an asset, so it will be taxed as such. However, since users can send and receive Bitcoin as currency, this raises other questions. When employees receive their paycheck in bitcoin, will it be subject to payroll taxes? If so, what will determine its rate in dollars? These and other issues will be resolved, eventually, but right now it's too early to guess what the future will look like.

When you look at the high volatility of Bitcoin's value against the dollar, this will not be an easy task. The value of Bitcoin changes by the minute, in some instances by the second. In addition, how will the IRS calculate payroll tax when Bitcoin is currently not recognized as an actual currency?

Legalities

Bitcoin presents several puzzles for court systems around the globe. The anonymity Bitcoin provides can prevent some individuals from being identified and prosecuted. Yet, even anonymity is not an insurmountable obstacle. Bitcoin-related Ponzi schemes have already been prosecuted under fraud and money laundering charges.

There are few examples at this point to show how Bitcoin will be handled in a court of law. In the United States, the IRS does not currently view Bitcoin as a currency; if a dispute were to arise surrounding Bitcoin, what would be the court's stance? We don't know, since few precedents exist. In a perfect world, a team of Bitcoin developers would work with law experts to establish Bitcoin's legal standing.

Fraud

At the same time fraud in its various forms has plenty of precedents in US courts. The Commodity Futures Trading Commission (CFTC) ruled in

November, 2018 against a hedge fund built around bitcoin. It turns out the defendant was running a Ponzi scheme.

A class-action lawsuit was filed in December, 2018 in California against a Chinese mining company. The defendant is accused of using the devices it sold to customers to mine cryptocurrencies for itself, while charging the customers for the energy usage.

Additional cases have been successful against individuals who default on bitcoin-based loans

Identifying Lawbreakers

How to provide anonymity while making it possible to identify individuals who are breaking the law is another contentious issue. This one, however, strikes at the very core of Bitcore's underlying philosophy. There are fears that in the future, bitcoin users will be required to register themselves. This would destroy entirely the very anonymity that makes the system so attractive. But that's all to be determined in the future.

Acceptance Rates In America

At this writing, only about six US states are openly opposed to cryptocurrencies. Currently, Connecticut, Georgia, Hawaii, Oklahoma, Washington and West Virginia have either outlawed or heavily regulated their use. For example, a law was passed in New York that requires businesses to acquire a BitLicense, if they wish to receive payments in bitcoin. The cost of applying for a BitLicense is so high however, that many companies have given up altogether the idea of accepting bitcoin payments.

American states vary wildly in their attitude toward cryptocurrencies. As of this writing, the following states have declared their acceptance of cryptocurrencies:
- Colorado
- Delaware
- Florida
- Illinois

- Kansas
- Montana
- Nevada
- New Hampshire
- New Jersey
- Texas
- Utah
- Vermont
- Virginia
- Wyoming

These states have either officially declined to regulate Bitcoin and its companions, or have legislated favorably toward its use.

The remaining American states are either undecided or are in the process of formulating legislation. It's unclear at this point whether they will be friendly or opposed to cryptocurrency transactions.

International Regulatory Threats

We also don't know what forms of regulation will be placed on bitcoin, as efforts to regulate it are on the increase. Depending on where you live and with which countries you perform your bitcoin transactions, you may have nothing to worry about for now, but watch out. As bitcoin continues to grow in popularity and economic impact, governments the world over can be expected to want a piece of the profits. You can expect to see changes in the future.

In countries such as the UK, Japan and the European Union, banks like Barclays and some government-run businesses have begun to accept bitcoin. While this seems to be an acceptance of the cryptocurrency, some are concerned that this may be an underhanded attempt to regulate – or outright own – bitcoin. If governments start to accept bitcoin payments, they could then bring laws into place to enforce how Bitcoin operates. As the future unfolds, how will Bitcoin continue its growth and avoid becoming a pawn of the governments where they do business?

International Legitimacy

In countries such as the UK, Japan and the European Union, banks like Barclays and even government-run businesses have begun to accept Bitcoin. While this would imply an acceptance of the cryptocurrency, some are concerned that this is an underhanded attempt to regulate it. If a government is willing to receive Bitcoin payments, will it more easily implement and enforce regulatory measures? It's too early to know how regulation will effect Bitcoin's economy. Only time will tell if Bitcoin is able to survive widespread regulation, if and when it occurs.

Bitcoin – The Next Gold?

Gold was originally considered the international trading standard. Instead of bartering for other goods, gold was the common denominator. Today Bitcoin has the potential to be the next overall standard of exchange, particularly since it has no connection to any single currency and is accepted across international borders. Bitcoin is a new type of commodity that carries many of the attributes found in the gold standard.

Gold does *not* derive its value from what a government says it is worth; rather, its value is based on what those using it *say* it is worth. Governments can assign it a value, but this value is subject to market fluctuations, all of which are based upon supply and demand.

While a dollar figure can be attached to bitcoin, its true worth is determined by the people who use it. Any dollar figure is simply an arbitrary representation of how much one entity *thinks* it is worth. Its actual worth is determined by what individuals are prepared to pay for it.

When we look at things this way, there is no doubt that bitcoin has the capacity to be the next form of gold, especially since it is not tied to any single currency. Plus, it's accepted across international borders. Bitcoin is a new form of commodity with the very traits needed for it to serve as the new gold standard.

Fresh Values For A New Age

This issue is not based on the fact that gold is an asset you can actually feel. Bitcoin possess a trait known as social capital. This refers to the power derived from individuals who adhere commonly to a certain set of values. Bitcoin goes beyond its existence as a form of currency; it is a movement. It's a movement against large financial institutions. It stands in opposition to tendencies by big government to cripple and simultaneously take over financial markets.

Now is the time the people can take back the power that was yielded to large organizations that centralized their services, gained a monopoly and then set prices at their own whim. Bitcoin's decentralized, open ledger system amounts to a movement, one that is gaining momentum daily.

Bitcoin will go on maturing and expanding in influence. It is already responsible for a revolution in computer technology by challenging existing hardware to perform ever more powerful calculations and by developing even more effective algorithms to solve critical challenges.

Regardless of Bitcoin's dollar value, its true worth lies within the movement it birthed to restore individual democratic control through decentralized transactions. This is where its true worth lies and will continue, on into the future.

Chapter 19: Online Resources

Because the field of cryptocurrency is ever-changing, with fresh innovations appearing daily, it is essential that you regularly supplement the knowledge gained in the book with online sources. The remainder of this chapter is devoted to providing you access to trusted sources where you can keep abreast of emerging technology and continue increasing your skills in various aspects of Bitcoin. We will discuss how you can regularly check online news and take advantage of traditional media channels. Finally, we will look at ways you keep up with all the latest Bitcoin trading news.

You will find plenty of online information about the blockchain, Bitcoin and the constantly shifting world of digital currency. While this book will get you started in fine style, your education is just beginning. The market continues to evolve and its landscape can change entirely, literally overnight.

Fortunately, you have a whole internet full of information at your fingertips. A simple search will turn up webpages tailored to your precise needs for information. The internet is your best source for up-to-date information on Bitcoin and all that it stands for. Personally, I have found the following news sources to be invaluable.

Bitcoin Wiki

Bitcoin Wiki is an independent and unbiased source where you can find plenty of current news regarding Bitcoin. You'll find it an invaluable commodity in the digital currency community, since it provides up-to-the-minute news on any changes, updated information on exchange rates and announcements of new services as they are available. Wikipedia is a commonly used source; it can explain the technology in as fine a detail as you require.

The Bitcoin Wiki covers everything: Satoshi Nakamoto's work, bitcoin nodes, mining and much more. I suggest you refer to it frequently; you'll learn plenty each time you visit.

Bitcoin Forums

Bitcointalk.org is a popular place for debates and service reviews. Although this bitcoin forum was created several years ago, it is consistently updated. Here you can find all the latest news about added goods and services, project development, etc. Anything you want to discuss is covered at Bitcoin Talk. You'll find the full range of opinions represented on the forum with plenty of room for lively debate!

Bitcoin Talk is not limited to Bitcoin. It also provides areas for the discussion of other digital currencies. You will find sub-forums available in a variety of languages.

Bitcoin Subreddits

If you are a user of Reddit, chances are you have already discovered subreddits while browsing online. I encourage you to explore; there are hundreds of subreddits threads touching on Bitcoin alone and many more cover every subtopic of cryptocurrencies you could imagine. These subreddits include discussions that range from the weird to the wonderful. You can find discussions about taking bitcoin into space next to explanations of why small fees are charged by bitcoin payment processors.

However, I should warn you; currently bitcoin subreddits are plagued by censorship. People are frequently banned and whole topics can be removed. Aside from this, it is still a decent place to find useful, practical information.

Here are a few Bitcoin subreddits to check out, for starters:
- Bitcoin for Beginners
- Bitcoin, but serious
- Bitcoin – The Currency of the Internet
- Bitcoin – The Internet of Money
- Bitcoin Mining Forums: Turning Computers Into Cash

Bitcoin.com and Bitcoin.org

Bitcoin.org is considered the home page of Bitcoin. Here you will find brief descriptions of various aspects of participating in bitcoin. They include demonstration videos and downloadable links for wallet software. The site manages to provide highly useful information in an easy-to-understand format that can be applied even by the complete beginner.

The phrase "bitcoin.com" ranks high among the most-searched-for phrases on internet search engines. Up until recently, bitcoin.com was a domain name that merely redirected people to a different site, but it has now become an expansive resource for all matters pertaining to bitcoin. It includes daily updated news reports and offers a range of opinions, all the better for gaining a glimpse of the big picture.

Bitcoin Blogs and Vlogs

No trend or niche can long stay relevant without dedicated sites that cover everything available on the subject matter. Multiple Bitcoin blogs have emerged. Many are run by hobbyists and – as such – may not be updated as frequently as the more "professional" sites. Still, you can gain valuable knowledge from both.

Because cryptocurrencies are still finding their place in the world, there is plenty of room for competition within news subjects. You'll find a variety of dedicated news sources available to feed your knowledge; www.coindesk.com and https://cointelegraph.com/ and https://insidebitcoins.com/ are just a beginning.

The field is so "busy" that the news releases are coming fast and furious at times; you'll benefit by frequently checking a Bitcoin-related site. Bitcoin is so different from everything that has gone before it that re-educating yourself will take time. Blogs and vlogs give users many angles on the same story. The crypto field is so complex and fresh discoveries are so frequent that it's essential to consult a variety of viewpoints before you can confidently present yourself as an expert. Each writer or videographer offers uniquely useful insights into a subject.

Mainstream News

The mainstream media have tended to view Bitcoin in a negative light, but as digital currencies continue to proliferate and Bitcoin continues to thrive, the situation is changing.

The technology behind Bitcoin is increasingly valuable to innovative companies looking for fresh ways to reach customers. Cryptocurrencies open up huge new market segments in the global marketplace for forward-thinking entrepreneurs. If you run any business, you'll want to keep your ears open to shifts in the international market, especially as countries develop their own policies that affect your ability to do business there.

Documentaries On Bitcoin

Multiple documentaries have followed Bitcoin from the very beginning. Most of them are free and easy to locate online. Most have not been created as money spinners, but to raise visual awareness and to allow everyday people to visualize ways Bitcoin can change their lives and how it is transforming the world around them.

Here are a few Bitcoin documentaries you may find helpful:
- Bitcoin: The end Of Money As We Know It
- Ulterior States
- The Rise And Rise Of Bitcoin
- Life on Bitcoin
- The Bitcoin Gospel
- Banking on Bitcoin

Charts And Maps

While most users are interested in bitcoin's value fluctuations, there's a lot more to this cryptocurrency than its exchange rate. There are several online sites where you can get the current price together with the average trading information and charts that show both the relevant buying and selling statistics. Here are a few sites you may find useful:

- Bitcoinwiscom.com – tracks real-time information gathered from a number of exchanges worldwide and distinguishes the major fiat currencies. The information is free for people to use and is kept right up to date. Coinmarket-cap also shows how the current market is capitalized by all of the digital currencies available.
- Fiatleak.com – lets you "see" transactions in real time. It's this presented in an easy-to-understand format. The site uses bitcoin symbols on a world map to show where in the world transactions are taking place at any point in time.
- Coinatmradar.com – shows where the cryptocurrency ATMs are located in each country in the world where they can be traded.
- Coinmap.org – also provides a world map that shows where you can exchange bitcoin. You can zoom down to the street level and pinpoint exchanges, including their contact information.

Chapter 20: The Big Picture

In this final chapter, I want zoom out from all the details we've been looking at and take in the overall Bitcoin landscape. Is bitcoin internet money? Is it an alternative currency? Is it a parallel financial system? Is it the basis for a different way of looking at life?

The simple answer is yes. As you must have already realized, Bitcoin is all of the above and so much more.

While it's becoming increasingly easy to use bitcoin, you must never forget that you are its primary guardian. Along with your total control of your bitcoin comes total responsibility for its safety. Even though it's now as easy to buy bitcoin as you can buy concert tickets or ice cream, your bitcoin is infinitely more valuable – and more powerful – than any of these and requires stronger forms of protection.

The Basics

Let's recap. Bitcoin is an alternative payment method that is currently attracting a great deal of media attention. It was created with the express purpose to provide a decentralized alternative to our current financial systems. Bitcoin provides full transparency for spending in the shape of a public ledger known as the blockchain. It uses a brilliant form of security entailing both public and private keys.

Buying

To be able to use bitcoin, you need to actually have some bitcoin. Unfortunately, obtaining bitcoin is not as easy as putting your card into an ATM. To acquire bitcoin:
1. Make sure the person or the platform you are using is legitimate, just as you would for other online transactions.
2. Use an exchange to purchase your Bitcoin. Next register your details on the exchange you have chosen, deposit your currency such as dollars or pound sterling, then complete the purchase at the current exchange rate.
3. Alternatively, you can always purchase bitcoin directly from another person.

Storing Bitcoin

The exchange storing your bitcoin is only ever as effective as the exchange's security. Although many users do choose this option, they are not in full control of their bitcoin while it resides anywhere but a wallet they own. You should only store your bitcoin at an exchange temporarily, when you are preparing to use it.

The best place to store your bitcoin is in your wallet. By using a software wallet, you can store and secure your bitcoin on your own computer. To ensure your bitcoin stay safe, you should encrypt your wallet and perform regular backups. Run virus checks on a regular basis and educate yourself in internet security. If this really is too much to absorb immediately, I would recommended using an online wallet until you are comfortable with the way they work. This will simplify the entire process for you.

If neither of these options serve your purpose you could use a paper wallet and send your bitcoin to an address that has no connection with an online exchange or to any software that your may have on your computer. This Bitcoin will only be available to spend when you manually redeem them using your private key.

Securing Bitcoin

Bitcoin security is just as important as the security with your regular bank account. By ensuring your bitcoin are secure, there is little likelihood of someone stealing them. Make sure your password is unique and not something that would be easy for others to guess. Don't use it any place else.

When you choose to use any kind of online service you should look for any two-factor authentication. This employs a second level of password that resets every minute or so using a smartphone or similar device. If you are offered this additional security, you should enable it immediately.

Mining

Bitcoin mining uses extremely fast computers to solve complex mathematical equations, which allow transactions to occur and pays the miners for their work. Without miners, no transactions are processed and there would be no confirmations given to validate you have genuine bitcoin. This would eventually lead to no new coins coming into circulation as no rewards would be on offer.

The Bitcoin network is secured and sustained by its participants. Individuals contribute by running a Bitcoin node, by providing a dedicated amount of computer power to aid the mining, and by transacting business in bitcoin.

To make your own mine, you can purchase the extremely expensive hardware-or you can employ a third party cloud-based service to mine for you.

Using Your Bitcoin

With bitcoin in hand, or in wallet, you can buy things. In addition to online transactions, a number of local shops are now willing to receive payment in bitcoin. Business owners enjoy major advantages when customers choose to pay in bitcoin for purchases.

Whether for long haul or short term, day trading or locking away in cold storage, even trading across various altcoins for a profit, you can utilize bitcoin just as you would any other form of investment. It contains the same opportunities and risks as any other highly speculative venture.

Using The Blockchain

This is where the present meets the future. As more blockchain-based applications appear, you will find your life gets easier. These apps can do everything from alerting you when the cookies in your oven are done to specifying the level of identification information you will reveal when a liquor store wants proof of your age. You can receive insurance claim payments rapidly and you can pass critical health information on to emergency responders, all thanks to information managed on the blockchain.

Conclusion

Congratulations! You are now well on your way to becoming an expert at Bitcoin. By working your way through this book you have taken a major step forward into the technology of the future. You now have enough knowledge to get started and enough additional resources at your fingertips to continue to grow your skills and keep abreast of new developments as they occur.

So, where do you go from here? I would recommend you continue to immerse yourself in research and application, learning from the bitcoin community and exploring ways Bitcoin can enhance your life and boost your business.

Use It

Your first step is to begin using Bitcoin! After all, you'll only start gaining experience if you use it. Start small and move out slowly if you want, but get moving.

Use Bitcoin:

- Pay for purchases in bitcoin whenever possible.
- If you own a business, let it be known that you are willing to receive payment in bitcoin.
- Pay friends back in bitcoin.
- Give bitcoin as gifts.
- Begin a bitcoin savings account.
- Pay your bills using bitcoin.
- Include bitcoin with your other investments.

Unless there is a major setback for Bitcoin, you can expect it to continue to mature and develop on into the future. Bitcoin is still leading the way in driving technology forward and you can expect additional technological advances to shake up your world and open up even more opportunities.

Finally, let me extend a very warm welcome to you as you enter the world of Bitcoin; I wish you the best while using it.

Thanks for reading.

If this book has helped you or someone you know then I invite you to leave a nice review right now. ***It would be greatly appreciated!***

My Other Books

For more great books simply visit my author page or type my name into the Kindle Store search bar or the Books search bar: **Susan Hollister**

Author Page

USA: https://www.amazon.com/author/susanhollister

UK: http://amzn.to/2qiEzA9

Thanks and Enjoy!

Made in the USA
Columbia, SC
16 August 2020